ANCIENT
MODERN

POLYMER CLAY + WIRE JEWELRY

Ronna Sarvas Weltman

 INTERWEAVE.
interweavestore.com

EDITOR: KATRINA LOVING
TECHNICAL EDITOR: JAMIE HOGSETT
DESIGNER: KARLA BAKER
PRODUCTION DESIGNER: KATHERINE JACKSON
PHOTOGRAPHER: DOUG YAPLE

Text © 2009 by Ronna Sarvas Weltman
Photography © 2009 by Doug Yaple
All rights reserved.

Interweave Press LLC
201 East Fourth Street
Loveland, CO 80537-5655USA
interweavestore.com

Printed in China by Asia Pacific Offset.

This page: *Eastern Burst.* From the private collection of the author.

Page 3: Top photo: *Copper Creek;* bottom photo: *Inside the Realm.* Both from the private collection of the author.

Page 8: *One World Necklace.* From the private collection of the author.

Page 9: *Interlude.* From the private collection of the author.

Library of Congress Cataloging-in-Publication Data

Weltman, Ronna Sarvas.
   Ancient modern : polymer clay + wire jewelry / Ronna Sarvas Weltman.
     p. cm.
Includes bibliographical references and index.
ISBN 978-1-59668-097-5 (pbk.)
1. Polymer clay craft. 2. Wire craft. 3. Jewelry making. I. Title.
TT297.W487 2009
731'.2--dc22

                    2009002231

10 9 8 7 6 5 4 3 2 1

acknowledgments

This book would not be this book without Doug Yaple's glorious photography. Thank you to my gracious, patient, wise, and literate editors: Tricia Waddell, Katrina Loving, Jamie Hogsett, Rebecca Campbell, and Nancy Arndt. Thanks also to book designer Karla Baker and production designer Katherine Jackson. Thanks to Susan Lomuto at dailyartmuse.com, muse to thousands. Thanks to jewelry artist Loretta Lam for the inspiration, the encouragement, and the long conversations about art, with forays into the care and feeding of teenage sons. Speaking of whom, I would not have been able to pull this off without my son Danny's astonishing computer skills, and I wouldn't have had as much fun without my son Robby's enthusiasm and encouragement. Mostly, thank you to my husband, Jordan, who frets endlessly about my wild rides sans roadmap but has never, ever asked me to put my foot on the brakes. What a guy.

For my parents, Maynard and Nettie Sarvas, with love and gratitude.

TABLE OF CONTENTS

{ INTRODUCTION }

LIKE MANY JEWELRY ARTISTS, I BEGAN MAKING JEWELRY BY STRINGING BEADS and stones and finishing off my necklaces and bracelets with clasps I found at the bead store. Soon, however, I found myself wanting to make more of my own mark on my jewelry, which led me to wire and later to polymer clay. I love working with materials that I can hold, wrap, bend, pinch, squish, indent, tweak, ball up, roll out, squish again, set aside, and go back to days, weeks, or even years later. I love the warmth, resonance, and substance that wire adds to a piece, and I find myself seduced by the infinite possibilities in color, texture, and shape offered by polymer clay.

I am particularly drawn to combining wire with polymer clay because while both mediums offer me the opportunity to craft primitive and even quirky designs, the combination achieves an aesthetic counterplay within each piece, adding to the visual intrigue. Although wire has little intrinsic color, it offers firm structure and a solid foundation. Polymer clay, on the other hand, offers so many possibilities with color, texture, and form. It offers an opportunity to take my art to a place where whimsy, imagination, and even folly can rule the day. People are often attracted to books, movies, and plays that offer multiple story lines within the plot, because that multidimensionality is what makes them intriguing. I think we respond to art in the same way. A piece of jewelry that can simultaneously evoke structure and whimsy, that can suggest a solid foundation coupled with a hint of folly, is going to engage and delight us on many levels.

True craftsmanship takes practice and experience. Every day I get an idea for a fabulous piece of jewelry. However, when I go into the studio to make it, sometimes it's all wrong. But I keep plugging away, and eventually I do hit the sweet spot and I really like whatever it is I eventually make. So don't get discouraged if not everything works out just the way you planned on your first attempt.

I hope you will use this book as a guide in helping you find your creative voice in jewelry design. Experiment. Explore. Be open-minded about using these materials to bring forth the exciting, delightful, original ideas that are percolating inside you. The jewelry you imagine is all right there, waiting for you to find an opportunity to blend creativity and craftsmanship with a deeper understanding of how to put it all together.

DESIGNING JEWELRY

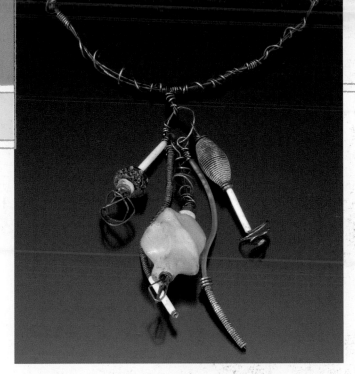

I DESIGN JEWELRY AS ART TO WEAR.
I want it to be beautiful but also durable, practical, and comfortable. All too often, jewelry design takes place on a tabletop and doesn't necessarily make the transition to wrist, neck, earlobe, or garment particularly well. The laws of physics —gravity, in particular—can play capricious tricks on designers. Taking the time to consider some of those challenges will allow you to design jewelry that looks as fabulous on the wearer as it does on the design table.

Designing jewelry often feels like a largely intuitive process, but a careful consideration of the principles of design will help you create more beautiful pieces, particularly when you're feeling stuck. Those principles include rhythm, balance, proportion, emphasis, harmony, and scale.

Rhythm, in the context of design, includes repetition and progression. Repetition is obvious in the photo at top right of one of my pieces, called *Interlude*. You can see that I used brass spacers in each of the dangle elements, creating a harmonious rhythm. Each of the dangles looks as if it is part of the whole because of the repeated use of the same elements. Progression, on the other hand, is a variation on repetition—it is an ordered, systematic sequence or transition, suggesting motion, which can be very dynamic. *Interlude* has five dangles hanging from a wire circle. When I first made the two long, thin dangles, they were straight. The necklace looked static. By curving them into undulating lines, but keeping the remaining three dangles straight, I created a progressing pattern of straight, curvy, straight, curvy, straight.

The free-form wire embellishment along the neck wire is similar in size and appearance to the free-form wire embellishment on the pendant, creating both balance and proportion. The necklace has an obvious focal point in the large center bead on the pendant, which creates emphasis. At the same time, the other embellishments are large enough that they don't get lost in the overall composition, which satisfies three of the principles; balance, proportion, and scale. At the same time, the color scheme is muted, which creates harmony.

These few examples explore how the design principles were used in this particular piece. Although I don't necessarily think consciously about the design principles when I'm working on a new piece of jewelry, my understanding of them informs all of the decisions I make. However, when I am struggling with a piece, the design principles become a more conscious part of the process. That is when I ask myself questions, perhaps about the balance I am achieving, or about whether there is too little, or too much repetition. As you become more familiar with these principles and find yourself using them in your jewelry design—both consciously and unconsciously— you will delight in the growth of your own creativity.

COLOR INSPIRATION

Color inspiration for organic jewelry can come from anywhere and anything. Nature, of course, is the primary source of inspiration for organic design; a walk in a lush garden or a trip to a public aquarium to look at undulating jellyfish, sea urchins, and other colorful life forms can spark your imagination. You can also find inspiration in everyday objects. One of my favorite sources of color inspiration is the *New York Times* Sunday Styles section. Books with beautifully photographed pictures of flowers, plants, tropical birds, and sea life are also rich sources of ideas for color and form.

Translating a source of inspiration into a color palette that is both energetic and harmonious can be challenging. The color wheel is a great starting point for determining color harmony. Colors that are next to each other on the color wheel are called analogous colors. An analogous color palette is, generally speaking, relatively more serene and relaxed. Colors that appear opposite each other on the color wheel are complementary, providing a high contrast to each other. Therefore complementary colors inject more energy into a color palette.

The color wheel may be too much of a good thing when you don't want to look at all colors but just want to figure out which colors you want to use for a particular piece of jewelry. I like to use books I call my "color cookbooks" (see Resources on p. 134). Although different in size and approach, they all offer harmonious color combinations in groups of two or more colors. Most artists find they gravitate to certain colors. Exploring and working with different color palettes will make you more open-minded toward options in your work, while also making you more attentive to the colors in your environment. When you are more attentive, you're much more open to inspiration. And inviting inspiration, more than anything else, will help you in your growth as an artist.

SUNSET'S RECOLLECTION The muted turquoise in the off-center focal bead is particularly dramatic because of its contrast to the reds and peach tones in this necklace. Notice that greens and blues are opposite reds and peach tones on the color wheel.

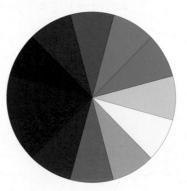

THE MECHANICS OF JEWELRY DESIGN

One of the luxuries of making your own jewelry is having the flexibility to size every piece according to your own tastes and needs. If you are making jewelry for others to wear, it is important to be familiar with common sizing terms and measurements. Even though the terms for sizing are consistent, bodies are less so. Be aware of this when you design for others and be sure to take appropriate measurements before beginning.

NECKLACES

Unlike other types of jewelry, necklaces have an added design challenge: a necklace sometimes just doesn't look as good hanging on a neck as it does during the design process when it's laying on a flat surface. Unfortunately, there isn't any magic formula to address this issue. Choker-length necklaces are a little less challenging because they're designed to simply ring the neck, while a

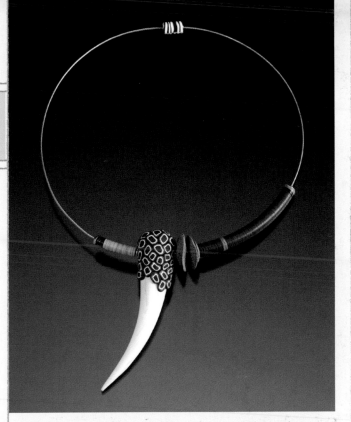

SHARP WORDS The focal bead in this choker is significantly heavier than the vulcanite heishi beads surrounding it, therefore it remains at center-bottom on the wearer's neck even though the design is asymmetrical.

STANDARD NECKLACE SIZES

COLLAR	Hugs the neck	14" (35.5 cm)
CHOKER	Fits at the base of the neck	16" (40.5 cm)
PRINCESS	Dips below the collarbone	18–20" (45.5–51 cm)
MATINEE	Hangs slightly above the chest	23–27" (58.5–68.5 cm)
OPERA	Hangs below the chest	35–37" (89–94 cm)

longer necklace includes a slope down onto a chest, with shoulders, collarbones, breasts, and all sorts of anatomical challenges affecting the drape of the necklace. Here are a few strategies to help you with this designers' quandary:

Don't ignore the laws of gravity

Think about where to put the hole in a pendant or focal bead. If you put the hole directly in the middle of a top-heavy element, it may flip over because of the weight at the top.

When designing necklaces, I often make the beads that are closer to the clasp with lightweight cores, but I make the focal bead—and sometimes the beads right next to it—out of solid polymer clay so that they are heavier and will therefore be more likely to stay at the bottom of the necklace.

Tell your clasp to stay put

Whenever possible, secure your focal element in place on the cable, chain, or cord it is hanging on so that it will stay put, and the clasp won't travel downward. If your focal element has wire, you can simply wrap the edges tightly onto the cable, cord, or chain. If you aren't using wire, then use a drop of cyanoacrylate glue or a dab of two-part epoxy glue to keep the focal element in place forever. See instructions on p. 22 for a method of attaching a clasp that I use frequently.

Don't ignore anatomy

Think about how beads will lie against the wearer's body. Many women have prominent collarbones. If your design includes branch-like elements you may want to limit them to the bottom of the necklace.

A choker of large beads will make the wearer's neck appear larger, so many women prefer necklaces that have an interesting focal element, but are strung on a narrow cable, cord, or chain. Chunky-bead chokers are one of my favorite styles, but be mindful that they are not universally popular or practical.

A WALK DOWN MADISON AVENUE The focal element of this bracelet is very light and therefore stays put on top of the wearer's wrist.

BRACELETS

A standard bracelet size is 7" (18 cm) but different wrist sizes may require adding or subtracting length from this base size. A difference of an inch or two in a necklace can often be negligible, but in a bracelet even ¼" (6 mm) can make all the difference. An ill-fitting bracelet can be annoying—uncomfortable if it fits too snugly and easily lost if it fits too loosely. Be careful to size bracelets according to the wearer's wrist size, leaving enough length for the bracelet to move easily on the wrist but not enough to slip off the wearer's hand.

The following strategies will help you design bracelets that work within the laws of physics as well as aesthetics:

Make the focal section lighter than the clasp

Because clasps are usually lightweight, it can be challenging to counterbalance them in the design process, particularly if you want to feature large beads in your bracelet. One way to address this is to use lightweight beads in the part of the bracelet that you want to sit on top of the wrist. Fortunately, polymer clay beads with foil, cornstarch packing peanut, or cork clay cores are lightweight, as are free-form, open-wire designs. When you design a bracelet with chunky beads, make the focal bead with a light core and make the beads closer to the clasp solid clay and/or larger and heavier wire beads. As an added bonus, using large lightweight beads also makes a bracelet more comfortable to wear. After all, who wants to be weighed down?

Metal-plated plastic beads are lighter than solid metal beads. Consider using lighter plated beads at the focal area of the bracelet and heavier solid metal beads closer to the clasp. Natural materials such as bone, seedpods, and wood all make lightweight and interesting materials for bracelets.

Make it stretchy

Bracelets strung on elastic cord hug a wearer's wrist and therefore stay in place. It still makes sense to be mindful of gravity and aim to make the focal area of the bracelet lighter, but you do have more flexibility when the bracelet is strung on elastic cord. Elastic cord also has another important asset—the wearer doesn't have to fumble with a clasp.

RINGS

I love big fat impractical rings. What makes a ring impractical? If it is higher than about an inch, you'll have trouble putting on and removing jackets and sweaters while wearing it. Ditto for bracelets with vertical embellishments. That said, sometimes you just want to have a little

HOPE'S GARDEN A wide shank provides a solid foundation, both structurally and aesthetically, for this fanciful ring.

fun with jewelry and make a statement, and rings offer the perfect opportunity to do just that.

Physics of ring design

The part of the ring that wraps around your finger is called the shank. If the shank is narrower than the focal embellishment, you run the risk of having the focal element slip down rather than staying upright because it is heavier than the shank. If you want to design a ring with a substantial focal embellishment, use a wide shank.

PINS

Pins are a lot of fun to design, and because they are, generally speaking, on a flat plane, you have fewer laws of physics that you need to pay attention to. But like every other kind of jewelry, you need to be mindful of the practicalities before you get to have fun with the aesthetic decisions.

Consider physics.

If you attach your pin back too low on the back of the pin, then the pin will be too top heavy and the top part of the pin will tip outward because gravity is pulling it down. Attaching the pin back higher up on the pin will ensure that it remains flat against the wearer's chest.

A heavy pin will pull lighter fabric down with it in its gravitational journey to the ground, so the lighter the pin, the more flexibility for the wearer.

Keep those back sides pretty, too

Metal pin backs aren't the prettiest things in the world, but you can make a small, thin sheet of polymer clay to lay over the portion of the pin back that attaches to the pin. Some polymer clay artists put a tiny stamp with their name or mark on their pin back covering.

EARRINGS

Earrings present fewer challenges because they can dangle; therefore you're working with gravity rather than fighting it. As long as an earlobe can comfortably hold the material it's appropriate for earrings, but polymer clay lends itself particularly well to earring design because it is so lightweight. Here are some tips and tricks to consider when designing earrings:

Think in terms of mirror images rather than exact duplication

If an earring design has a curve or bend or is asymmetrical, consider how it hangs in the earlobe so you can determine whether the two earrings need to match exactly or whether a design element requires that one earring be a mirror image of the other.

Watch out for metal sensitivity

Most people are able to wear sterling silver ear wires, but some people are sensitive to metals that contain nickel and copper. Surgical stainless steel, titanium, niobium, and 14-carat gold or gold-filled wires are the best alternatives for sensitive wearers.

Include ear wires in the design process

Make the ear wire part of the design, giving it as much intentionality as the rest of the earring. For overall beauty, take the extra time to design an ear wire that is not only utilitarian but is part of the overall design.

SWEET AND ROUND The slight variation in shape and dramatic variation in texture keep this repetition of circles visually engaging. The subtle texturing on the back orb was created by cupping my palm and then pressing it onto the clay.

ABOUT WIRE

If you are inexperienced in working with wire, buy some inexpensive craft or copper wire for practice and experimentation. The high price of silver and gold wire has also motivated many artists and crafters to explore colored craft wires. You may find yourself getting inspiration from the many colors and finishes of craft wire, and its affordability makes experimentation realistic and rewarding.

WIRE GAUGE

Wire is measured in thickness, or gauge. The larger the number of the gauge, the smaller the diameter of the wire; 12-gauge wire is much fatter than 26-gauge wire. Sometimes you can let your eye be the judge of what size wire to use, but when you're working on a project that calls for a specific gauge of wire you can use the chart at right to help you identify the gauge (if the spool is not marked).

The projects in this book have recommended wire gauges. However, because each gauge has different properties, I encourage you to experiment with different gauges, observing how a design evolves when the materials change.

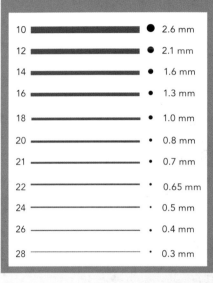

WIRE GAUGE CHART

Gauge		Diameter
10		2.6 mm
12		2.1 mm
14		1.6 mm
16		1.3 mm
18		1.0 mm
20		0.8 mm
21		0.7 mm
22		0.65 mm
24		0.5 mm
26		0.4 mm
28		0.3 mm

Flat-nose pliers

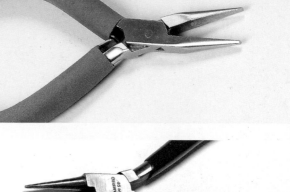

TOOLS

Investing in some quality wireworking tools can make a noticeable difference in your work. Well-made plier handles let you grip your wire more easily and therefore get a smoother curve or sharper bend. A heavier, sturdier hammer will give you more bang every time you strike your wire or metal. It is also a better investment because it will last longer. Fortunately, you don't need a lot of tools to get started.

Flat-nose pliers have broad, flat jaws. Use them for holding and gripping wire and making sharp bends. They're also useful for opening and closing jump rings.

Chain-nose pliers can often be used interchangeably with flat-nose pliers. Because they have pointed ends, they're useful for getting into tight spots and tucking in wire ends.

Round-nose pliers have long, conical jaws and are used for making loops and rounded bends in wire.

Mandrels are forms used to shape metal and, although they are not absolutely necessary, you will find them useful if you will be creating a lot of jewelry.

A ring mandrel is used to shape wire or clay into a ring shape, but you may find it easier to shape your wire or clay over a dowel because some ring mandrels are not stepped and will yield a ring shaft that is smaller on one end.

Chain-nose pliers (top) and Round-nose pliers (bottom)

Ring mandrel

A bracelet mandrel (not pictured) will help you form bracelets that fit gracefully onto a wrist.

A necklace mandrel (not pictured) is shaped like a neck and will help you create necklaces with proper drape.

Ball-peen hammer

Texturing hammer

Dapping die (wood block) and dapping punch (silver tool)

Flush cutters

Flush cutters are used to cut wire and make a flush (flat) cut on one side of the wire, while leaving the other side pointed. If you would like both ends of the wire to be cut flush, you may want to invest in a double-flush cutter instead. Do not use flush cutters on memory wire because they will ruin your cutters; instead, purchase memory-wire cutters to cut memory wire.

A **ball-peen hammer** is used to flatten metal (wire or sheet) but will leave marks. When I either don't mind or intend to make marks, the ball-peen hammer is wonderful. If the head is formed from hardened steel, it will be harder than the metals you are working with and will therefore stay free of mars, chinks, and other injuries to its head. This is important because a hammer that has any dents or imperfections will impart those imperfections to your metal.

Texturing hammers have interesting textures on them for imprinting on metal. Keep in mind that your favorite texturing hammer could be an old hammer that has been scratched, dented, and deformed. Such a surface could be ideal for creating organic designs on wire and sheet metal; however, specific textures are also available.

A **dapping die** is used for doming round metal disks. You can buy wooden or metal blocks with a variety of sizes of circular depressions. **Dapping punches** have rounded tips. A metal disk is put into the circular depression and then hammered with the punch. Depending on

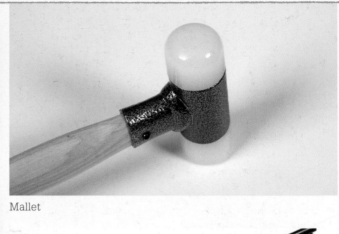

Mallet

Two-hole punch

WEDNESDAY NIGHT ON MARS Sometimes just a little wire can have a lot to say. This wire was given slight curves and turns, then flattened with an extra flare at the end, giving a graceful and delicate touch to this otherwise robust design.

the thickness and hardness of the metal disk, you can either use the punch like a hammer or use a hammer to pound on the punch.

A **bench block** (pictured on p. 19) is made of hardened steel and is used for pounding metal. I prefer using a small one, because at any one time I'm only pounding a small surface of whatever I'm working on. I also recommend getting a bench block pad, a cushion that diminishes the noise you make when you pound metal on a bench

block. It also absorbs the shock of pounding, and therefore keeps the bench block from moving.

A **mallet** is used when you want to harden metal without marking or flattening it. Mallets, which often have heads comprised of or covered with rawhide or nylon, have larger and softer surfaces than ball-peen hammers.

A two-hole punch is used for making holes in sheet metal and wire that has been pounded flat.

TIPS FOR TEXTURING WIRE:

- If you want to flatten wire without texturing it, take your time—tap softly and evenly and use the rounded face of the hammer. Be sure to file down any sharp edges or points that are created as you flatten or texture the wire. If the wire is thin, you may find a paper fingernail file easier to work with.

- Pounding harder, coming from an angle rather than a straight up-and-down motion, and using the edges of the hammer face will yield the texturing nicks and dents that can make wire look more interesting and organic.

- It is easier to texture wire before it has been shaped into a piece of jewelry, but pounding wire also causes it to work harden, which means it becomes stiffer and stronger. Work hardening is an important step in the wire-jewelry process because it ensures that your wire creation will keep its shape. However, once the wire is work-hardened it will stiffen and become harder to work with. If you want to texture your wire after it is already bent into a design, use round-nose pliers to put kinks, bends, and marks into the wire.

- Don't limit your texturing to wire. You can give other components and findings, even tiny jump rings, interesting textures that will add to your finished piece.

Files (not pictured) are indispensable to ensure that your jewelry has no sharp edges. In the case of ear wires, it's not simply a matter of aesthetics or comfort. A sharp point on the end of an ear wire could puncture a tender earlobe. File the edges of your wire, either with a cup bur (also called a wire rounder), which has a cup-like file end for rounding ear wires, or by simply using a small file to round the ends. If most of your metalwork is wire, you can get by with a few small files.

WIRE TECHNIQUES

Here are some techniques that will allow you to coax the character and beauty out of your wire, adding unique touches to your jewelry.

Texturing

When you purchase wire, it is smooth. Texturing, which gives wire character and personality, is accomplished by banging, pounding, distorting, and smashing. It really is that simple. Banging wire with the rounded end of a ball-peen hammer will yield a different texture from pounding it with the edge of the flat side. Practice on a piece of copper wire, which will respond similarly to silver wire but will cost you a lot less.

Creating a patina

Using liver of sulfur to antique, or darken, sterling silver and copper wire makes the wire look more organic and can enhance any texturing you have done.

Liver of sulfur is made from potassium sulfides. I have read and heard opposing opinions about its toxicity—that it is quite toxic and, alternatively, that it is perfectly benign. I recommend taking precautions when using it, if for no other reason than to avoid smelling up your studio or house. If you are concerned about disposing of the solution when you are finished, you can place it outside and it will neutralize after a few days.

19

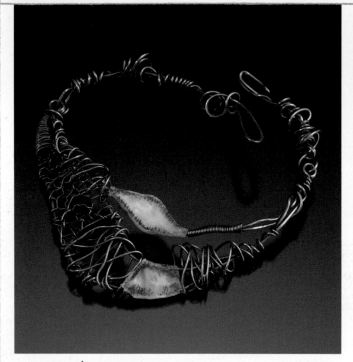

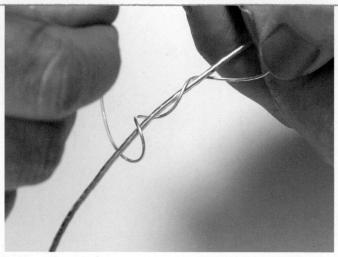

CAVEGIRL'S BLING Antiquing copper wire with liver of sulfur and adding brown shoe polish to the polymer clay gave this contemporary creation a prehistoric patina.

Liver of sulfur is remarkably easy to use. Drop a pea-sized nugget into about a cup of hot water. It will quickly dissolve. Then simply dip your silver or copper into the solution. The hotter the water and the more liver of sulfur in the solution, the more quickly the wire will darken, but you need only a tiny bit of liver of sulfur to do the job. After the silver or copper is darkened, rinse it under running water. Then use #0000 steel wool to buff the black from the surface. Afterward, you can buff it again with a polishing cloth or toss it in a tumbler to restore shine to the surface. If your finished piece will include something like leather or fabric cord that you don't want to dip into the solution, be sure to antique the wire before assembling the piece.

Coiling Wire

Coiling wire is the process of wrapping wire around another piece of wire called the base wire. Coiled wire can be wrapped very uniformly and evenly around the base wire or loosely and unevenly, depending on the look you want to achieve.

To coil wire, hold the base wire in your nondominant hand and wrap the coiling wire around it with your dominant hand. If you are right-handed, you will be coiling from left to right. I find it easier to leave a tail of a few inches on the left to grasp, particularly as I'm beginning the coil. The direction is reversed for left-handers.

The Coiling Wire chart on p. 21 will help you estimate how much wire you need when making uniform coils. If you want to coil 28-gauge wire around 12-gauge wire, for example, the 28-gauge wire would be your coiling wire and the 12-gauge wire would be your base wire. Find 12-gauge wire in the left column and the 28-gauge wire in the right column, and you will see that you need about 18¾" (47.5 cm) of 28-gauge wire for every 1" (2.5 cm) of 12-gauge base wire. The tension and spacing of your coils will affect the amount of coiling wire you use.

	28-GAUGE COILING WIRE	26-GAUGE COILING WIRE	24-GAUGE COILING WIRE	22-GAUGE COILING WIRE	20-GAUGE COILING WIRE	18-GAUGE COILING WIRE	16-GAUGE COILING WIRE	14-GAUGE COILING WIRE
BASE WIRE (PER INCH)								
12-GAUGE BASE WIRE	18¾" (47.5 cm)	19" (48.5 cm)	16" (40.5 cm)	13¼" (33.5 cm)	11⅛" (28.5 cm)	9½" (24 cm)	8¼" (21 cm)	6⅞" (17.5 cm)
14-GAUGE BASE WIRE	15⅝" (39.6 cm)	15¾" (40 cm)	13⅛" (33.3 cm)	11⅜" (28.7 cm)	9⅜" (23.8 cm)	8⅛" (20.6 cm)	7⅛" (18 cm)	6½" (16.5 cm)
16-GAUGE BASE WIRE	13" (33 cm)	13⅛" (33.3 cm)	11½" (29 cm)	9⅝" (24.4 cm)	8⅛" (20.6 cm)	7¼" (18.5 cm)	6½" (16.5 cm)	
18-GAUGE BASE WIRE	11" (28 cm)	11⅜" (28.9 cm)	9½" (24 cm)	8¼" (21 cm)	7" (18 cm)	6⅜" (16.2 cm)		
20-GAUGE BASE WIRE	9⅜" (23.8 cm)	9¼" (23.5)	8½" (21.5 cm)	7⅛" (18 cm)	6⅜" (16.2 cm)			
22-GAUGE BASE WIRE	8⅜" (21.3 cm)	8¼" (21 cm)	7" (18 cm)	6¼" (16 cm)				

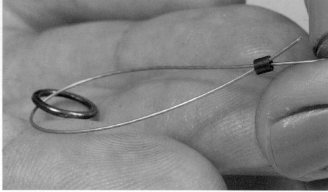

FIGURE 1

Creating Clasps

Some of the necklace projects in this book are strung on Soft Flex beading wire that is affixed to sterling silver closed (soldered) jump rings with crimp tubes (for attaching the clasp). Follow the instructions below to attach the jump rings.

Finishing a necklace so that a clasp can be attached:

1 Leave at least 6" (15 cm) of beading wire on each side of the strung beads.

2 String a crimp tube onto one end, loop the beading wire through a jump ring and then bring the beading wire back through the crimp tube and one or more beads in the necklace (**Figure 1**).

3 Pull the loop so it is tight and then nudge the crimp tube right up against the jump ring. Using either flat-nose or chain-nose pliers, tightly press on the crimp tube to squeeze it flat (**Figure 2**).

4 Snug the beads up against the jump ring.

5 Repeat Steps 1–4 on the other side of the necklace, making sure the beading wire is pulled tight so it doesn't show after both sides are crimped. Snip any extra beading wire flush against a bead hole so the beading wire doesn't show.

FIGURE 2

FIGURE 3

Clasp variations

6 Attach a clasp to one of the jump rings, the other jump ring will be the ring portion of the clasp (**Figure 3**).

Whenever possible, I like to hide my crimp tubes. They can be hidden easily and attractively by coiling wire over them, which then becomes part of the overall design of the necklace or bracelet.

FIGURE 1

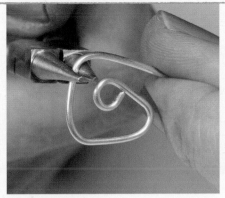

FIGURE 2

FIGURE 3

FIGURE 4

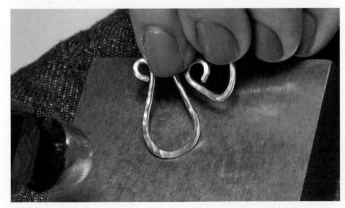

FIGURE 5

Basic Clasp:

1 Using 14-gauge or heavier wire, make a small loop around the tip, or narrow end, of your round-nose pliers (**Figure 1**).

2 Make a larger, loose loop around the small loop (**Figure 2**).

3 With your larger loop pointing outward, make another curve of the same size going in the opposite direction. Cut your wire above the top of the clasp as shown (**Figure 3**).

4 Bend the end of the wire just cut outward, making a small loop around the tip of your round-nose pliers, as in Step 1 (**Figure 4**).

5 Flatten the large curves on your clasp by placing it on a steel bench block and gently pounding with a hammer (**Figure 5**).

Once you understand how to make a basic clasp, you can make endless variations. Instead of making the loose loop in Step 2, you can make sharp bends to create squares and triangles, or softer ovals rather than round circles. You can achieve interesting variations simply by flattening the wire more in some areas than in other areas. Extra flattening where the wire curves and bends can be particularly intriguing. Take some time to practice with some copper or craft wire, and you will find that you are soon a master of clasp improvisation and composition.

ABOUT POLYMER CLAY

Polymer clay is a form of polyvinyl chloride (PVC) mixed with liquid plasticizers that remains workable until it is cured by baking. I use Premo clay, which was developed for artists, because it is easy to manipulate and is extremely strong after curing. Polymer clay can be set aside and then picked up again after a very long time—even several years later if it's kept away from heat and direct sunlight.

Before you work with polymer clay, you need to condition it. You can do so by rolling it through the thickest setting of a pasta machine about ten times. Alternatively, you can roll it into a rope in your hand, twist the rope, roll it into a ball, and then create a rope again; repeat the process about ten times until the clay feels softer and more pliable. Or you can simply keep squishing it a bunch. Some colors are stiffer than others, and some older polymer clay may be stiffer and need more conditioning. Warmer clay is also easier and quicker to condition. If you're working with several new packages of clay, you can warm them up by putting them against your skin. You can even sit on them to warm them up—your body being the ultimate low-tech warming tool.

TOOLS AND MATERIALS

Not only are most of the tools for polymer clay relatively inexpensive, but you may already have some of them in your kitchen, your tool cupboard, and even your junk drawer.

Tissue blades are vital for making clean cuts, particularly when you're cutting slices from canes. One side is sharper for cutting and slicing and the other side is blunt so you can rest your hand on it. A tissue blade is very sharp; take care when you work with it so you don't

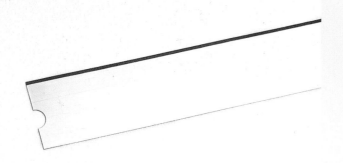

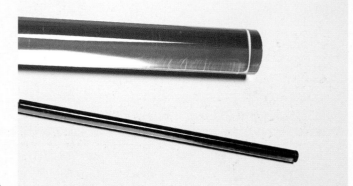

Tissue blade

Acrylic rollers

cut your fingers. Some manufacturers notch the blunt side so it's easier to distinguish.

Acrylic rollers are used to flatten and smooth your polymer clay. I use a 1" (2.5 cm) roller for most sheets of clay, and a ½" (1.3 cm) roller for smaller pieces. You may prefer using a brayer, which is a roller with a handle.

A **Lucite square** is a handy tool for rolling evenly shaped logs of clay and for flattening clay without leaving fingerprints. Hold the square parallel to your work surface and roll the clay beneath it to form a log or press down to flatten. Although they are not a well-known polymer clay tool, and therefore usually unavailable in art supply or craft stores, you can obtain them readily from online polymer clay resources (see p. 134).

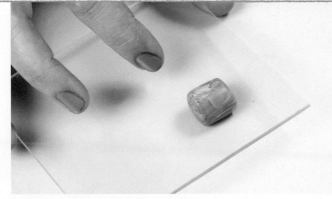

Lucite square

Pasta machine

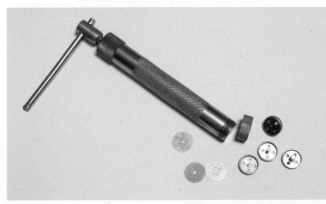

Extruder

A **pasta machine** has two metal rollers that squeeze the clay into sheets as it is rolled between them. The space between the rollers can be adjusted with a dial on the side to make the sheet thicker or thinner, as desired. Although it isn't necessary to have one, a pasta machine is a great tool to have, especially if you plan to work extensively with polymer clay.

Ball styluses (not pictured) are useful for making evenly rounded indentations in clay and also for smoothing clay in small spots. Ball styluses are available with different size balled ends.

An **extruder** is essential for several of the projects in this book. If you've ever made cookies with a cookie press or used a caulking gun, the concept is the same. Clay is loaded into the barrel of the extruder and a disk is affixed to it. As the clay is extruded, it takes the shape of the hole in the disk. You can also attach a core disk to extrude hollow cords.

Light bulbs (not pictured) make fabulous molds for bead caps and bell shapes. Because their glass surface is so smooth, you don't even need to use a release agent. Embed your light bulbs in scrap polymer clay so they will stand up in the convection oven.

Needle tools (see p. 32 for usage instructions) are used to poke holes in uncured beads and for texturing. The metal handle makes this tool a little heavier and therefore more effective, but you can use a wooden skewer or even a toothpick to poke holes and carve ridges in uncured clay if you wish.

Linoleum carving tools can also be used to create holes in cured beads. Simply hold the U- or V-shaped blade against the cured polymer clay and turn. It works like a drill, but you can do it slowly, making it easy to control.

Glass or marble cutting boards (not pictured) are my favorite surfaces for working with polymer clay because they won't get scratched by a tissue blade. You have many other options, however, including the self-healing cutting boards found in most grocery stores,

ABOUT POLYMER CLAY

parchment baking paper, or even waxed paper. Don't use anything textured or porous because the polymer clay will pick up its texture or stick to it.

Antiquing pigments and acrylic paints (not pictured) are often used to achieve a faux patina by painting the surface of a cured piece, rubbing the pigment or paint into crevasses in the clay, then wiping it off the surface.

Shoe polish (not pictured) can be applied to polymer clay with an inexpensive firm paintbrush to achieve a beautiful faux patina and subtle sheen.

Metallic powders (not pictured), also called embossing powders, add a metallic or pearlized effect to polymer clay. They usually come in small jars and can be found in many colors. Use an inexpensive soft paintbrush to apply the powder and be aware that a little powder goes a long way, so use it sparingly. Always use a face mask when you apply metallic powders to avoid inhaling the microscopic particles.

Liquid polymer clay (not pictured) forms a strong bond when you combine cured and uncured polymer clay or two pieces of cured clay. The liquid clay must be cured because it does not act as a glue until it is cured; it then forms a permanent bond. I have found that leaving the polymer clay and liquid polymer clay to sit for about 24 hours before curing allows the liquid polymer clay to "set," forming a stronger bond. If your pieces will not stay together while curing, you may need to prop them with polyester fiberfill or aluminum foil or use a drop of cyanoacrylate glue (below) for a temporary hold.

Cyanoacrylate glue (not pictured), such as Zap-A-Gap and Super Glue, can be used to attach pieces of clay to each other, cured or uncured. Because they bond instantly, the first bond is the strongest, so trying to move the pieces after bonding them will compromise the strength of the bond. Extreme care needs to be taken when you work with cyanoacrylate glue because if you get it on your skin or in your eyes, it will bond instantly.

Two-part epoxy glue (not pictured), which hardens after you mix the two parts together, forms the strongest bond for gluing polymer clay to nonporous surfaces such

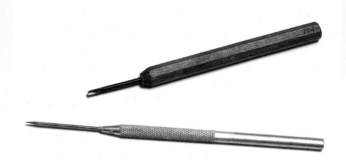

Linoleum cutter (top) and needle tool (bottom)

as metals and glass. You can purchase quick-acting and slow-acting epoxy glues. Quick-acting epoxies are more convenient when you want a quick bond, whereas slow-acting gives you more time to move your piece around to get things right. Slow-acting epoxies are stronger, but even the quick-acting epoxies will probably be strong enough for all your needs. Epoxy glue has strong noxious fumes, so use it in a well-ventilated area and be careful not to lean directly over it while using.

CURING POLYMER CLAY

Use a separate, dedicated convection oven (not a microwave) for baking polymer clay. Although polymer clay is certified as nontoxic, put the oven in a well-ventilated area, either close to a window or out in the garage. Raw and properly cured polymer clay is nontoxic, but if polymer clay is burned, the fumes are toxic. If you do accidentally burn the clay, open your windows to air out the fumes and avoid re-entering the area until the fumes are gone. A large convection toaster oven will maintain more even baking temperatures, which is very important. Some ovens may get spikes in temperature, but the fan in a convection oven means the air inside circulates more, resulting in a more even temperature. Larger is better because the farther away the clay is from the heating element, the less likely it is to get burned.

Premo should be cured at 275°F (130°C) in a preheated oven for 30 minutes per quarter inch of thickness. You know how leaving cookies in the oven too long causes them to burn? That doesn't happen with polymer clay. As long as you are curing it at the right temperature, you cannot burn it. In fact, baking it longer will strengthen it even more.

Never rely on the temperature gauge of the oven to be correct. Invest in an oven thermometer to ascertain the correct temperature. Set the oven dial to 275°F (130°C) and then check the oven thermometer. Adjust the dial up or down as needed to achieve the correct temperature and then keep the dial at that setting. Because some ovens tend to spike over the desired temperature and then come back down, it's a good idea to put your clay into a preheated oven.

One of the lovely things about 275°F (130°C) is that it's not hot enough to burn paper. Therefore, you can put your uncured polymer clay onto a piece of paper and put it into the toaster oven. Although paper does not burn at these low temperatures, it is important to make sure that neither your paper nor any other material is touching the heating element.

SURFACE EFFECTS

It is astonishing how many things can be done to the surface of polymer clay. You can imprint it with molds and textures, add paint and powder, even add inclusions such as seeds, salts, and spices. You can texture and color it after it has been cured by carving into it, rubbing paint into crevasses, smoothing and polishing with wet/dry sandpaper, and adding shoe polish or other waxes to give it shine and color. The possibilities are infinite. Every time I work with polymer clay, I spend a little time experimenting with surface techniques.

Texturing polymer clay

When I design organic jewelry, I find my inspiration for texture in nature. I want my jewelry to have the same sense of serendipity that is found there, so I aim to freely combine bits of this and pieces of that.

You can purchase texture plates and stamps in just about any texture or design you can imagine. Some of the projects in this book include texture pads and stamps (see Resources on p. 134). You can also use many materials already at your fingertips—literally—for texturing. One of my favorites is the inside of my palm, which gives me even more dramatic prints than my fingertips. Sandpaper is another favorite texturing material. I also use pieces of interesting fabrics, screens, and even bits from old tools.

You can also make your own texture plates and stamps. You can carve or press a texture into some polymer clay, cure it, and voilà! you have a unique texture stamp of your own. Whether you make your own molds or stamps out of polymer clay or use purchased texture molds and stamps, you need to use a releasing agent to prevent the polymer clay from sticking. If you are going to cure the clay in the mold, use cornstarch as a releasing agent and simply wash it off the cured clay after it is finished baking. Water is an effective release agent when the clay is going to come away from the mold before it is cured.

FIGURE 1   FIGURE 2   FIGURE 3

You can also use two-part silicone molding compounds to make your own molds, texture plates, and stamps. The advantage to using two-part silicone instead of polymer clay is that the two-part silicone is more flexible than the clay and releases the clay more easily. It can also be cured, so if you want to mold a very thin sheet of clay onto a texture, for instance, you can leave it on the mold while it cures without worrying about distorting it as you pull it off the mold.

To make your own molds:

1 Combine equal parts of a molding compound and blend thoroughly **(Figure 1)**.

2 Working quickly, spread the compound over the texture you wish to mold. I like to smooth the back side of the mold evenly, so I can use it as a "texture" to get smooth finishes **(Figure 2)**.

3 Let it set up (harden) according to the manufacturer's recommendation and then peel away from the texture after it has hardened completely **(Figure 3)**.

The fingerprint controversy

If you work with your bare hands, you will get fingerprints on your clay. You may feel this adds authenticity, or it may drive you crazy. There is no right or wrong opinion on this.

The easiest and quickest way to eliminate fingerprints is to wear latex gloves. Because I can't stand the feel of latex gloves, I save them for the very last step in the finishing process. If I'm making round beads, for instance, I make the beads with my bare hands, including rolling them into a round ball. Then I don my gloves and give them a few more rolls to eliminate the fingerprints. Ditto for smooth disks: I make little balls with my bare hands, but then when it comes time to squish them into disks I wear the gloves.

Because your aim in wearing latex gloves is to eliminate marks on the clay, be sure your gloves are snug. Wrinkles in loose-fitting gloves will make marks on the clay, so if your hands are small, buy small gloves.

MARBLING

There is no mystique to marbling polymer clay. You simply put different colors of clay together and blend them by rolling them in your hands or using an acrylic roller or a pasta machine. It's easy to get a fabulous marble if you pay attention to these pointers:

- Pay attention to how colors will combine. Green and purple, for instance, can sometimes be fun together, but blend them together and you get mud.
- Finally—and perhaps most important—keep blending. Yes, sadly, if you blend too much, you'll end up with a solid color, and it can be difficult to judge when you've passed the point of no return, but the vast majority of people will stop blending too soon. So take a risk—run it through the pasta machine again . . . and again.

Blending clay into colors

Different colors of polymer clay can be blended together to form new colors in the same way paint colors are blended to create new shades. Blend red and yellow, for instance, to get orange. You can use colors straight from the package without blending, but blending colors together lets you achieve more nuanced effects. Adding a little bit of white to most colors will achieve a "creamier" look, which can be quite beautiful. Adding translucent polymer clay will give more depth. Inks used for stamp crafts can also be blended into the clay to achieve subtle or dramatic effects.

CANES

Many of the techniques used in working with polymer clay evolved from ancient lampwork-glass techniques. Canes are simply logs of clay that are made to be sliced

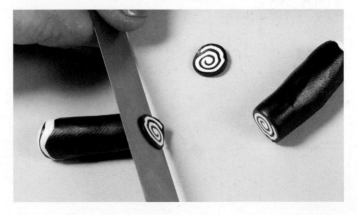

- Always use colors that look good together. If the colors that are being blended are not harmonious, the marble blend won't look good.
- Be sure to include dramatic contrasts. If all the colors in a marble blend are similar, it may be boring. All of my marbled blends have either black or white in them, and most have both.
- Pay attention to the color saturation levels of different clays. A little black, for instance, goes a lot further than a little white. Use highly saturated colors in significantly smaller proportions to other colors.
- Experiment with using translucent clay, which adds depth to marble blends, particularly if the beads are polished with shoe polish or wet/dry sandpaper after baking or dipped in an ice-water bath to increase the translucent polymer clay's transparency.

ABOUT POLYMER CLAY

up so the slices can be used as embellishment, much as lampwork bead artists use glass canes to create embellishments. Canes can be very simple; for example, you can simply roll a thin log of black clay, slice circles from it and use them to embellish a polka-dot bead. Canes can also be very complex. Some polymer clay artists make extremely intricate geometric canes evoking kaleidoscopes, flowers, animals, and even human faces that delight and astonish.

Leeching

One of the reasons polymer clay lends itself to designing organic art and jewelry is that you can use its properties to mimic nature, such as the rough, jagged edges found in some stones and tree barks. You can sometimes get this effect simply by rolling unconditioned clay through the pasta machine. In fact, one of the easiest ways to gauge whether your clay is well-conditioned is by observing the edge of the sheet as it rolls out of the pasta machine. If the edge of the sheet is smooth, the clay is probably well-conditioned. If the edge is rough and jagged, the clay probably needs to be run through some more.

If you want to create a jagged edge, you can create one by leeching the clay. Leeching the clay dries it out. Roll out a thin sheet of clay and place it between two sheets of white paper. Rub the paper so it adheres to the clay. Leave it overnight or longer, and when you return to it you'll see the paper has absorbed some of the moisture from the clay. Run the leeched clay through the pasta machine and you'll get craggy edges, which can be a fabulous effect.

Although sharp edges can make very dramatic jewelry, getting poked isn't fun. So if you are designing something such as a bracelet bangle that will be worn against bare skin, gently give the edges an outward curve by grasping them between your thumb and forefinger and turning them upward so the pointed edges nip the air instead of tender skin.

MAKING LIGHTWEIGHT BASE BEADS

I dislike wearing heavy jewelry, so I do my best to make all of my jewelry as light as possible. Although polymer clay beads are lighter than just about any other bead, a necklace filled with fat polymer clay beads will obviously be more comfortable if it is lightweight. You can make your beads lighter by forming them over lightweight base beads molded from air-dried cork clay, aluminum foil that has been crumpled and molded into a ball, or dissolvable cornstarch packing peanuts, which are not only ridiculously lightweight, but can be dissolved to make your bead completely hollow. When you are forming a bead over a core, roll the clay for the bead into a sheet using the

TIPS FOR CHOOSING THE RIGHT BASE BEAD MATERIAL

- Use a dried cork clay or aluminum foil base bead when you want round beads. After you have covered the base bead with polymer clay, poke a hole where you will be completing the bead hole after the bead is cured to release any trapped air.

- Use cornstarch packing peanuts when you want a very organic, irregular shape and also want hollow beads. You can press several cornstarch peanuts together if you wish to form a larger base bead. Use a tiny drop of water to get them to stick together and molded into a circle shape, but be aware that too much water will dissolve them. After the beads are cured, you can leave the cornstarch peanuts in if you wish, but sometimes the material makes it difficult to thread beading cord through the bead. If that's the case, just immerse the bead in water to saturate the core, which will dissolve. Put your mouth over one hole and blow the cornstarch out. You may need to immerse it again and blow more to get all the material out.

thickest setting of your pasta machine, cut it into circles or pieces to cover the core, apply it to the base bead, and roll into a ball.

MAKING UNIFORM BEADS

When creating a symmetrical design, you'll save yourself time and grief by making uniform, lightweight base beads. To get uniform-size beads, roll out a log of cork clay and mark it off with a ruler or the Kato Marxit, a six-sided ruler that impresses even marks onto a cane or sheet of clay. Slicing the log at equal intervals will ensure that your beads will be of uniform size, and will make it easier to keep everything symmetrical.

MAKING ROUND BEADS

Rolling a round bead is another one of those skills that can be intimidating if you've never tried to roll a round ball, but once you get it you've got it forever. You can purchase a bead roller, but I promise that if you just practice for a little while, you'll master it.

Rolling round beads:

1 Make a round bead by rolling a piece of clay in the middle of your palms. Cup your hands slightly. A bigger bead will naturally make you cup your hand more.

2 Move both of your hands to shape the bead. Sometimes beginners don't realize they're only moving one hand and keeping the second stationary. As soon as you start moving both hands at the same time, you will have a much easier time rolling a round bead.

3 Toss the bead around inside your palm so you're pushing at it from all different angles. At first this movement will be conscious, but after you've practiced you'll do it so quickly and subtly that it will be one even motion as part of the rolling motion.

BAKING ROUND BEADS

When you are baking round beads, you cannot put them onto a flat piece of paper or they will have a flat spot after they are cured. Cure round beads in a paper fan (a piece of paper folded into a fan). The beads rest inside the V without actually touching the bottom, so they stay round. Another option for round beads is to place them on a piece of polyester fiberfill quilt batting, which is also safe in a 275°F (130°C) oven. Because the fiberfill acts as a cushion, the bead doesn't sit on a flat surface, so it stays round.

Increasing durability

When you take your beads out of the oven, place them in ice water for a few moments. This will harden the polymer even more. An ice-water bath also makes translucent clay more transparent and strengthens liquid polymer clay's attachment properties.

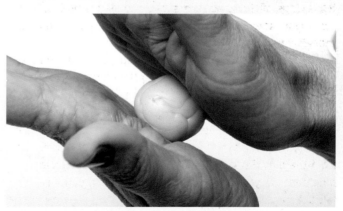

FIGURE 1

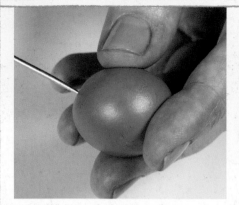

FIGURE 1

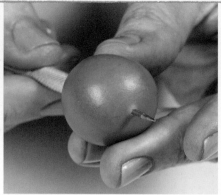

FIGURE 2

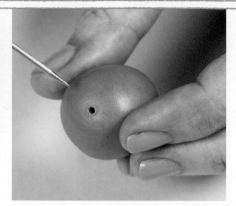

FIGURE 3

POKING HOLES IN BEADS

For most of the projects in this book, you can poke holes before or after curing beads. The advantage of poking holes before curing is that the clay is still soft and pliant, so it's quick work. Also, if you put the hole in the wrong place, you can usually re-form the bead, cap, or disk. However, it's also possible to distort uncured clay when poking holes. Waiting to cut a hole until after the bead, cap, or disk is cured eliminates the worry over distortion, but there is no room for error.

To use a needle tool:

1 To make a hole that goes through the center of an un-cured bead, gently grasp the bead in your nondominant hand and, holding the needle tool in your dominant hand, lightly place the point of the needle tool on the spot where you want the hole.

2 Place the index finger of your nondominant hand on the bead, at the spot on the bead where you want the needle tool to emerge (opposite the spot where you've placed the tip of the needle tool; **Figure 1**).

3 Gently twist the needle tool back and forth as you push it into the bead. The gentle twisting keeps the clay from sticking to the needle tool, and therefore keeps the bead from distorting by being flattened. Aim the

needle tool toward the middle of your index finger (placed on the bead in Step 2).

4 When you feel the little poke from the needle tool on your index finger, gently grasp the bead between your thumb and index finger and twist the needle tool so it goes through the bead completely **(Figure 2)** and then pull it back out, still using a twisting motion.

5 Turn the bead over and push the needle tool through the opposite hole, again using a twisting motion. This will smooth the hole on the opposite side. It is impor-tant to have a smooth hole on both sides of the bead because if a bead is placed on any fiber, elastic, or leather cording, a rough hole could fray it **(Figure 3)**.

MAKING BEAD CAPS

Bead caps can be made very easily using a light bulb to achieve the desired shape.

To form a bead cap:

1 Roll a round bead of polymer clay.

2 Place the bead on top of a light bulb or other round surface and pat the clay down to form a pod shape.

3 After curing, gently run a needle tool under the edges to loosen the bead cap from the mold.

{ HOW TO USE THIS BOOK }

Each project in this book features step-by-step instructions, supplemented with photos of the process to make the instructions easy to follow. There are many techniques used, both for wire and polymer clay, that are not broken down into steps for each project. For information on wire techniques, see About Wire on pages 15–23. For information on polymer clay techniques, see About Polymer Clay on pages 24–32. You will find a wealth of information on those pages, including some step-by-step instructions, tips and tricks to make the process smoother, and lists and explanations of tools and materials used for wire and polymer clay respectively.

Note: Items within the instructions that appear inside of parenthesis should be completed the indicated number of times. For example, string (1 accent bead and 1 Hemisphere bead) twice. This example indicates that 1 accent bead, 1 Hemisphere bead, 1 accent bead, and 1 Hemisphere bead should be strung (p. 129).

Other helpful sections include:

Designing Jewelry, p. 9

An explanation of art principles and how to apply them to jewelry design.

Color Inspiration, p. 10

A discussion of sources for color inspiration, as well as a brief introduction to the color wheel.

The Mechanics of Jewelry Design, p. 11

A breakdown of important things to consider when designing necklaces, bracelets, rings, pins, and earrings. This section includes helpful suggestions for obtaining correct fit, as well as useful pointers for creating beautiful and practical pieces.

Glossary, p. 129

Features illustrated instructions of the basic wirework techniques and knots used throughout the book.

PROJECTS

The order of projects begins with what I consider to be the simpler pieces, using techniques that are relatively easy and are perfect for getting your feet wet. The projects progress using increasingly challenging techniques to help you to expand and perfect your wirework and polymer clay skills.

As you advance through the book, you will find that many of the projects present the perfect opportunity for experimenting and learning new ways to combine wire and polymer clay to fabulous effect. Whether you are new to polymer clay, or wire, or both, you can be sure that you will find plenty of information to jump right in. And for those of you who already have experience, don't worry, there are plenty of wonderful unique and challenging surprises in the following pages.

SERENDIPITY'S SISTER
{ NECKLACE }

THIS NECKLACE IS A POTPOURRI OF COLORS and textures as well as polymer clay techniques. The primitive wire spacer beads serve as a unifying counterpoint to this colorful extravaganza. The challenge and the satisfaction in designing a piece like this is the consideration given to texture, color, and shape in each bead and deciding where each should be placed.

Finished Size: 20" (51 cm)

MATERIALS

Polymer clay in black, white, translucent, orange, ultramarine blue, purple, cadmium yellow, gold, turquoise, white pearl, and crimson

5 aluminum foil or cork clay 19mm base beads

Cornstarch packing peanuts

Brown shoe polish

White antiquing medium or acrylic paint

10' (4.3 m) of sterling silver 20-gauge wire for spiral beads

4' (1.2 m) of sterling silver 16-gauge wire for spiral beads (each spiral bead takes about 12" [30.5 cm] of wire)

10" (25.5 cm) of sterling silver 14-gauge wire for clasp

2 silver 8mm soldered jump rings

2 silver 2mm crimp beads

24" (61 cm) of .019 beading wire

TOOLS

Pasta machine or acrylic roller

½" (1.3 cm) thin acrylic roller

Tissue blade

Needle tool

Sharp point such as a second needle tool or a toothpick

Extruder

Firm paintbrush

2" (5 cm) diameter round light bulb to use as a mold

Assorted texture tips, mats, and/or stamps

Wooden skewer or thin dowel

Flat-nose or chain-nose pliers

Flush cutters

Latex gloves

Liver of sulfur

#0000 steel wool

Soft polishing cloth

necklace

Orange and Lavender Beads

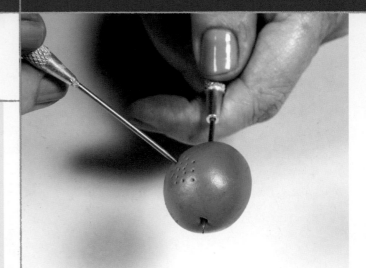

FIGURE 1

COLOR RECIPE

ORANGE BEAD:

1 part orange polymer clay

½ part white polymer clay

1 pinch of black polymer clay

LAVENDER BEAD:

6 parts white polymer clay

2 parts ultramarine blue polymer clay

1 part purple polymer clay

½ part black polymer clay

1. Mix clay for the Orange Bead, according to the Color Recipe above and roll out a sheet on the thickest setting of the pasta machine.

2. Squish two cornstarch packing peanuts together to form a lumpy ball. You can add a drop of water to act as a glue to keep them together.

3. Cover the packing-peanut ball with the Orange Bead clay (mixed in Step 1). Roll it in your hand like you're rolling a ball. It will be lumpy since the packing-peanut core is lumpy.

4. Poke a hole through the bead with the needle tool. Keeping the bead on the needle tool to hold it in place, use a second needle tool or other sharp point to poke little holes all over the bead (**Figure 1**).

5. Cure for 30 minutes.

6. Repeat Steps 1–5, using the clay mixture for the Lavender Bead according to the Color Recipe above.

FIGURE 2

FIGURE 3

Polka Dot Bead

7 Roll out a flat sheet of translucent clay on the thickest setting of the pasta machine. Be sure the sheet of clay is large enough to cover one of the 19mm cork clay or aluminum foil base beads. Mold the translucent clay sheet over the base bead and roll it into a round bead.

8 Make little dots of varying sizes out of black clay. Lay the dots on the surface of the bead very gently so you can move them around if you need to finesse the placement **(Figure 2)**.

9 When the dots are placed where you want them, pat them down to adhere to the bead and then roll them into the surface of the bead by rolling the bead between your palms. Wear latex gloves to achieve a smooth surface **(Figure 3)**.

10 You can either poke a hole in the middle of the bead with a needle tool or use a linoleum cutter to create one after it has been cured. Cure for 45 minutes.

Bumpy Ochre Bead

COLOR RECIPE

BUMPY OCHRE BEAD
1 part cadmium yellow polymer clay
½ part gold polymer clay

11   Mix clay according to the Color Recipe above for the Bumpy Ochre Bead and roll out a flat sheet on the thickest setting of the pasta machine.

12   Squish two cornstarch packing peanuts together to form a lumpy ball. You can add a drop of water to act as a glue to keep them together.

13   Cover the packing-peanut ball with the Bumpy Ochre Bead clay (mixed in Step 11). Roll it in your hand like you're rolling a ball. It will be lumpy since the packing-peanut core is lumpy.

14   Poke a hole through the bead with the needle tool. Keeping the bead on the needle tool to hold it in place, make indentations with a texture tool. The bead featured here was textured with a texture tip from the Cooltools Scatterbrained set **(Figure 4)**.

15   Cure for 30 minutes, cool, and apply the brown shoe polish with a firm paintbrush. Rub off the excess shoe polish with a soft cloth or paper towel.

Polka-Dot Hemisphere Bead

COLOR RECIPE

1 part cadmium yellow polymer clay
1 part gold polymer clay

16   Mix clay according to the Color Recipe for the Polka-Dot Hemisphere Bead above and form a bead cap over a light bulb.

17   Texture with a texture plate. The bead cap featured here was textured with the Cooltools Cheese Cloth texture plate.

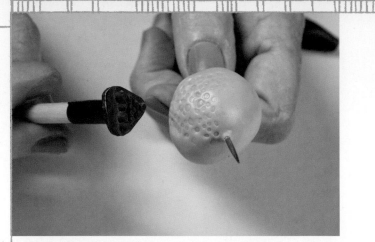

FIGURE 4

FIGURE 5

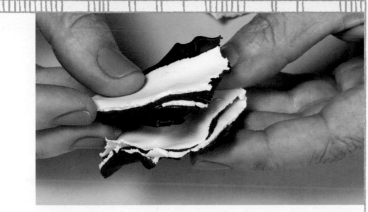

FIGURE 6

FIGURE 7

FIGURE 8

18 Poke a hole in the middle of the bead cap with a needle tool. Cure for 15 minutes and cool.

19 After the bead cap has cooled, remove it from the light bulb.

20 Fill the bead cap with translucent clay and flatten the surface with your fingers, making sure the translucent clay butts up against the rim of the bead cap **(Figure 5)**.

21 Make little dots of varying sizes out of red clay. Lay the dots on the surface of the bead very gently so you can move them around if you need to finesse the placement, as was done in Step 8 **(Figure 2)**.

22 When the dots are placed where you want them, push them into the surface of the bead, adhering them to the translucent clay and flattening them against the surface. Use latex gloves or roll a narrow acrylic roller over the surface of the bead to achieve a smooth surface.

23 Poke a hole through the middle of the bead with the needle tool, starting at the hole in the cured cap. Cure for 45 minutes.

24 Apply brown shoe polish with a firm paintbrush. Rub off the excess shoe polish with a soft cloth or paper towel.

Zebra Cane Bead

Note: The steps below describe the process for making a zebra cane, which simply consists of stacking one color on top of another, cutting them in half and stacking again, repeating the process until they have the amount and thickness of stripes you want, and occasionally "squishing" the layers to achieve the distortion that occurs naturally in zebras.

25 Roll out black and white sheets of clay on the thickest setting of the pasta machine.

26 Place the sheets on top of each other to form two layers. Cut or tear the layered clay in half and then place one half on top of the other so that you have doubled the layers of alternating colors. Cut in half again and place one half on top of the other so you again double layers of alternating colors **(Figure 6)**.

27 Pinch the stacked clay in a few places so the lines are no longer straight (**Figure 7**).

28 Cut that block in half and layer again and then repeat. Congratulations! You now have a zebra cane (**Figure 8**).

29 Cut slices from the side of the zebra cane and press them onto the base beads (**Figure 9**). Roll the slices into the surface of the bead by rolling the bead between your palms.

30 Poke a hole in the middle of the bead with a needle tool. Cure for 45 minutes.

Rivers and Eddies Bead

COLOR RECIPE

RIVERS AND EDDIES BEAD:
1 part turquoise polymer clay
½ part white polymer clay

31 Mix clay according to the Rivers and Eddies Bead Color Recipe above and roll out a flat sheet on the thickest setting of the pasta machine.

32 Squish two cornstarch packing peanuts together to form a lumpy ball. You can add a drop of water to act as a glue to keep them together.

33 Cover the packing-peanut ball with the Rivers and Eddies Bead clay (mixed in Step 31). Roll it in your hand like you're rolling a ball. It will be lumpy since the packing peanut core is lumpy.

34 Poke a hole in the bead with a needle tool. Keeping the bead on the needle tool to hold it in place, use a second needle tool or other sharp point to scratch little grooves into the clay. Sometimes it's easier to work from the base of the bead toward the middle; start from the bottom of the bead and then flip the bead over on the needle tool and work from the other end, again going toward the middle. You can use the point of your tool to carve out little grooves and

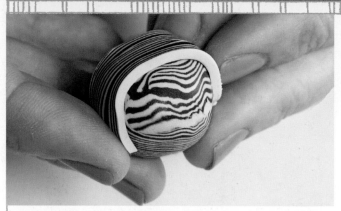

FIGURE 9

FIGURE 10

also lay the needle tool on the clay and rock it back and forth to form other grooves (**Figure 10**).

35 Cure for 30 minutes.

36 After the cured bead has cooled, apply brown shoe polish with a firm paintbrush just on the surface. Keep the inside of the grooves free of the shoe polish so the contrast is more dramatic. Rub off the excess shoe polish with a soft cloth or paper towel.

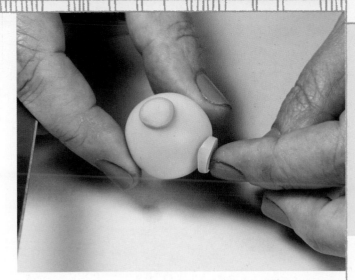

FIGURE 11

Ringed Beads

COLOR RECIPES

YELLOW-RINGED BEAD:

1 part translucent polymer clay

¼ part cadmium yellow polymer clay

CANE COVER:

1 part cadmium yellow polymer clay

1 part gold polymer clay

RED-RINGED BEAD:

1 part translucent polymer clay

1 part white polymer clay

37 Make a marble mix according to the Color Recipe for the Yellow-Ringed Bead above. Roll it flat on the thickest setting of the pasta machine and cover one of the 19mm base beads. Roll into a round bead.

38 Mix the clay for the Cane Cover according to the Color Recipe above, then make a simple cane by rolling a log with the leftover marble mix and cover it with a thin sheet of the Cane Cover mix.

39 Cut thin slices from the cane. Lay the slices on the surface of the bead (made in Step 37) very gently so you can move them around if you need to adjust the placement **(Figure 11)**.

40 When the slices are placed where you want them, roll them into the surface of the bead by rolling it between your palms. Use latex gloves to achieve a smooth surface.

41 Poke a hole in the middle of the bead with a needle tool and then cure the bead for 45 minutes.

42 Allow the bead to cool, then apply brown shoe polish to the bead with a firm paintbrush. Rub off the excess shoe polish with a soft cloth or paper towel.

43 Repeat Steps 37–42, using the Color Recipe for the Red-Ringed Bead above to create a marble mix for the bead in Step 37. Use the leftover marble mix for the simple cane formed in Step 38, but cover it with a thin sheet of crimson clay instead of the Cane Cover mix previously used.

SERENDIPITY'S SISTER NECKLACE

Marbled Bead

COLOR RECIPE

MARBLED BEAD:

1 part crimson polymer clay

½ part translucent polymer clay

¼ part white polymer clay

⅛ part black polymer clay

44 This is simple! Make a marble blend according to the Marbled Bead Color Recipe above and roll out a flat sheet using the thickest setting of the pasta machine.

45 Squish two packing peanuts together to form a lumpy ball. You can add a drop of water to act as a glue to keep them together.

46 Cover the packing-peanut ball with the marble blend (created in Step 44). Roll it in your hand like you're rolling a ball. It will be lumpy since the packing-peanut core is lumpy.

47 Poke a hole through the bead with the needle tool. Cure for 30 minutes, cool, and apply brown shoe polish with a firm paintbrush. Rub off the excess shoe polish with a soft cloth or paper towel.

Extruded-String Hemisphere Bead

COLOR RECIPE

EXTRUDED-STRING HEMISPHERE BEAD:

1 part cadmium yellow polymer clay

1 part gold polymer clay

48 Mix clay according to the Extruded-String Hemisphere Bead Color Recipe above and extrude a long string, using the smallest hole attachment on the extruder.

49 Starting at the center, wind the string onto a light bulb to create a bead cap, leaving a space in the center for a bead hole. Gently pat the strings to help them adhere to each other.

50 Cure for 15 minutes.

51 Fill the cooled bead cap with black polymer clay, creating a flat, smooth surface. Poke a hole through the bead with the needle tool.

52 Cure for 40 minutes, cool, and apply brown shoe polish with a firm paintbrush. Rub off the excess shoe polish with a soft cloth or paper towel.

Bumpy Teal Bead

COLOR RECIPE

BUMPY TEAL BEAD:

1 part turquoise polymer clay

1 part white pearl polymer clay

½ part gold polymer clay

53 Mix clay according to the Bumpy Teal Bead Color Recipe above and roll out a sheet on the thickest setting of the pasta machine. Then follow Steps 12–14 on p. 38, covering the packing peanuts with the Bumpy Teal Bead clay mixture. In Step 14, texture the bead by making dots with the flat end of wooden skewer.

54 After the bead is cured and cooled, use a brush, soft cloth, or your fingers to rub the surface with white antiquing medium or acrylic paint, then immediately lightly wipe the paint off with a cloth or paper towel so it remains in the crevasses, while allowing the clay to show through on the surface. Set the paint by curing for another 15 minutes.

String Bead

COLOR RECIPE

STRING BEAD:

1 part cadmium yellow polymer clay

1 part gold polymer clay

55 Make one 20mm round bead according to the String Bead Color Recipe above. Poke a hole through the bead with a needle tool.

56 Extrude a long, narrow string of clay using the leftover String Bead clay from Step 55. Holding the uncured round bead on a needle tool, lay strings of clay over the surface of the bead horizontally between the holes (**Figure 12**). Tap them down gently so they stick to the bead and tear them off near the edge of the bead, allowing them to overlap a little onto the needle tool. Continue laying strings of clay until the bead is covered, taking care not to make the strings perfectly straight but a little "bent" or "wiggly" so the bead has movement. If some strings break while you're laying them down—no problem! You want a primitive, organic look (**Figure 13**).

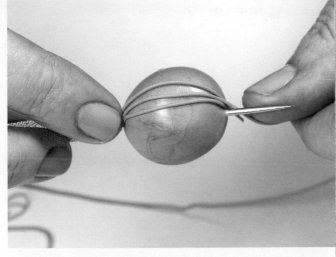

FIGURE 12

FIGURE 13

57 Before curing, use the tissue blade to cut the clay strings off at the edge of the bead so you have flush ends. Do this by holding the bead on the needle tool in your nondominant hand and holding the tissue blade in your dominant hand. Slowly turn the needle tool so the bead turns. As it is turning, make little cuts with the tissue blade so the strings are cut off and they lay even with the bead hole (**Figure 14**). Gently press them to attach them firmly.

58 Cure for 45 minutes, cool, and apply brown shoe polish with a firm paintbrush. Rub off the excess shoe polish with a soft cloth or paper towel.

Primitive Wire Beads

59 Begin to coil wire around a wooden skewer or thin dowel, wrapping down to the length of your desired bead (mine were about ⅜" [1 cm]). The wire should be wrapped firmly enough around the skewer so it doesn't slip, but you don't need to get the coils snugly next to each other as this part of the bead will be covered (**Figure 15**). This allows you to save wire and make the bead lighter.

60 Once you've coiled the length you want, continue coiling but wrap back over your coils so that your wire is now criss-crossing the first coils. Wrap loosely, in a nonuniform way with the wires crossing over each other (**Figure 16**). Make your coils at a slight angle to the first coils, so you start to get interesting "directions" in the pattern that starts to emerge.

61 Continue coiling, going almost to the end of the bead, but before getting to the end, reverse again, so you're wrapping back and forth. The rounder you want your bead, the more you'll wrap toward the middle of the bead (building up more wire in the middle will create a rounder bead). When you're happy with your bead shape, use the flush cutters to cut the wire close to the bead. Then use your chain-nose pliers to tuck the wire end into the bead so you don't have any sharp points sticking out (**Figure 17**).

FIGURE 14

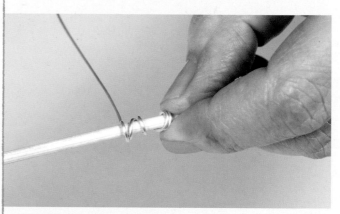

FIGURE 15

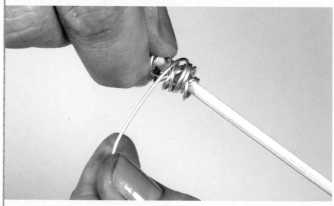

FIGURE 16

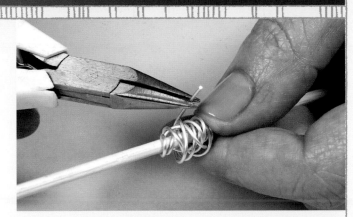

FIGURE 17

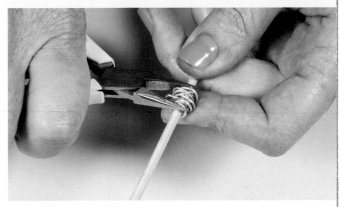

FIGURE 18

62 Repeat Steps 59–61 nine times with 20-gauge wire and four times with 16-gauge wire for a total of fourteen wire beads. If some of the beads are longer than you wish, you can squeeze them tighter horizontally with flat- or chain-nose pliers to shorten the length (**Figure 18**).

63 If you've used antiqued wire for the beads, buff the surfaces with #0000 steel wool to remove excess black. If your wire isn't antiqued, use liver of sulfur (p. 19) to antique the beads, then buff with #0000 steel wool and polish with a soft cloth.

Clasp

64 Use chain-nose pliers and 14-gauge wire to form the Basic Clasp on p. 23. Modify the design of the clasp if desired according to the instructions on p. 23.

Assemble the Necklace

65 Attach one end of the clasp to one jump ring. Use the beading wire to string (p. 129) 1 crimp bead and the jump ring used in Step 64. Pass back through the crimp bead and flatten with flat- or chain-nose pliers. String 1 Primitive Wire Bead, the Orange Bead, 1 Primitive Wire Bead, the Polka Dot Bead, 1 Primitive Wire Bead, the Bumpy Ochre Bead, 1 Primitive Wire Bead, the Polka Dot Half-Bead, 1 Primitive Wire Bead, the Zebra Cane Bead, 1 Primitive Wire Bead, the Rivers and Eddies Bead, 1 Primitive Wire Bead, the Red-Ringed Bead, 1 Primitive Wire Bead, the Lavender Bead, 1 Primitive Wire Bead, the Marbled Bead, 1 Primitive Wire Bead, the Extruded-String Half-Bead, 1 Primitive Wire Bead, the Bumpy Teal Bead, 1 Primitive Wire Bead, the Yellow-Ringed Bead, 1 Primitive Wire Bead, the String Bead, 1 Primitive Wire Bead, 1 crimp bead, and the other jump ring. Pass back through the crimp bead and flatten with flat- or chain-nose pliers.

NIGHTFALL IN MOZAMBIQUE
{ NECKLACE }

THIS NECKLACE FEATURES A STARK CONTRAST in colors, along with a sense of movement and energy supplied by variations in shape, texture, and pattern. The complexity in the design is enhanced by the liberal use of translucent polymer clay, which adds depth to many of the marble blends and canes.

Finished Size: 20" (51 cm) long.

MATERIALS

Polymer clay in black, white, burnt umber, and translucent

Brown shoe polish

12' (3.6 m) of black 19-gauge steel wire for wire ball bead

10" (25.5 cm) of 14-gauge wire for clasp

50 brass 6mm spacer beads

2 sterling silver 8mm closed (soldered) jump rings

2 silver 2mm crimp beads

24" (61 cm) of .024 Soft Flex beading wire

TOOLS

Pasta machine or acrylic roller

½" (1.3 cm) thin acrylic roller

Needle tool

Tissue blade

2" (5 cm) diameter round light bulbs to use as molds

Extruder

Ball stylus

Round-nose pliers

Flat- or chain-nose pliers

Flush cutters

Latex gloves (optional)

Liver of sulfur

#0000 steel wool

Polishing cloth

Firm paintbrush

necklace

Circle-Embellished Beads

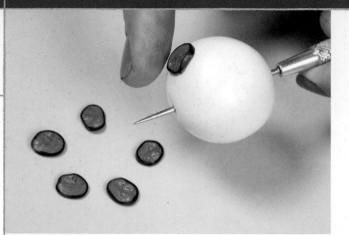

FIGURE 1

COLOR RECIPE

MARBLE MIX:

1 part translucent polymer clay

¼ part white polymer clay

LIGHT CIRCLE BEAD:

1 part translucent polymer clay

1 part white polymer clay

DARK CIRCLE BEAD:

1 part translucent polymer clay

¼ part burnt umber polymer clay

¼ part white polymer clay

⅛ part black polymer clay

1   Make a cork clay or aluminum foil 20mm base bead; set aside. Create a marble mix according to the Marble Mix Color Recipe above. Roll it flat on the thickest setting of the pasta machine and cover the 20mm base bead. Roll between your palms to form a round bead.

2   Make a cane by making a marble mix according to the Dark Circle Bead Color Recipe above and covering it with a thin sheet of black clay. Cut thin slices from the cane.

3   Poke a hole through the bead with the needle tool. Keeping the bead on the needle tool to hold it in place, lay the slices of cane on the surface of the bead very gently so you can move them around if you need to adjust the placement **(Figure 1)**.

4   When the slices are placed where you want them, roll the bead very lightly and briefly so the slices do not blend into the base bead.

5 Cure for 45 minutes, then allow the bead to cool. Apply the shoe polish with a firm paintbrush and then rub off the excess with a soft cloth or paper towel.

6 Repeat Steps 1–5 for a second Circle-Embellished Bead, but make the cane in Step 2 according to the Light Circle Bead Color Recipe and cover with a thin sheet of white clay.

Striped-Band Bead

7 Make a 20mm base bead of translucent clay and poke a hole through it with the needle tool.

8 Combine a few small pieces of black, white, and translucent scrap clay and run through the pasta machine to create a marble mix.

9 Cut a thin strip following the vertical stripes in the marble mix (**Figure 2**).

10 Holding the base bead on the needle tool, wrap the strip of striped clay around the bead. Tap gently to affix the band to the base bead but still keeping a gentle touch so the band looks like it is sitting on top of the bead (**Figure 3**).

11 Cure for 45 minutes.

12 Apply the shoe polish with a firm paintbrush and then rub off the excess with a soft cloth or paper towel.

Ring Bead

Note: Read entire step before continuing.

13 Repeat Steps 1–5 (on p. 48) twice to create a Ring Bead but make the cane in Step 2 with leftover Marble Mix from Step 1 and cover it with a thin sheet of black clay. In Step 4, blend the slices into the bead by rolling the bead between your palms. Use latex gloves to achieve a smooth surface.

FIGURE 2

FIGURE 3

Black Hemisphere Beads

14 Using a light bulb as a mold, form a bead cap of black clay onto the bulb. If you want the cap to be smooth, wear latex gloves to smooth the surface or use a thin acrylic roller to smooth it. Use a ball stylus to form gently rounded indentations all over the cap (**Figure 4**). Poke a hole in the middle of the bead cap with a needle tool.

15 Cure for 15 minutes. After the cap has cooled, remove it from the light bulb.

16 Fill the cap with translucent clay and smooth the surface. Poke a hole through the middle with a needle tool.

17 Repeat Steps 19–21 for a second Hemisphere Bead.

18 Cure both beads for 40 minutes.

Black Hole Hemisphere Beads

19 Repeat Step 19, using translucent clay instead of black.

20 After making the indentations, put a tiny round dot of black clay into each indentation and gently press down on each dot with the ball stylus so it fills the indentation (**Figure 5**).

21 Cure for 15 minutes. After the cap has cooled, remove it from the lightbulb.

22 Fill the cap with black clay and smooth the surface. Poke a hole through the middle with a needle tool.

23 Repeat Steps 24–27 for a second hemisphere bead.

24 Cure both beads for 40 minutes, then apply shoe polish with a firm paintbrush. Rub off the excess with a soft cloth or paper towel.

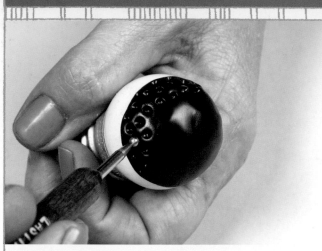

FIGURE 4

FIGURE 5

FIGURE 6

FIGURE 7

FIGURE 8

Cane-Banded Bead

25 Make a 20mm base bead from translucent clay and poke a hole through it with the needle tool.

26 Use the leftover cane from the Ring Bead on p. 49 or make another cane using the same colors from Steps 1 and 2. Gently press down on the cane so that it is slightly flattened (**Figure 6**). Cut slices from the flattened cane and lay them on your work surface.

27 Holding the base bead on the needle tool, use a tissue blade to lift the cane slices off the work surface and place them onto the bead, forming a band (**Figure 7**). Once you are happy with their placement, pat them firmly to affix the band to the base bead, but still keeping a gentle touch so you don't distort the canes.

28 Cure for 45 minutes and then apply shoe polish with a firm paintbrush. Rub off the excess with a soft cloth or paper towel.

Wrap-Capped Bead

29 Extrude a long, narrow string of black polymer clay.

30 Make a 20mm base bead from translucent clay. If you want it to be smooth and free of fingerprints, wear a latex glove for the final rolling.

31 Poke a hole through the bead with the needle tool and keep the bead on the needle tool.

32 Holding the bead perched on the needle tool, rub a few drops of liquid polymer clay onto the area where you will be attaching the string.

33 Lay the end of the extruded string next to the top hole of the bead, then gently tap the extruded string flush against the hole so it stays put.

34 Carefully turn the bead around and let gravity help the rope wrap itself around the tip of the bead, forming a bead cap (**Figure 8**). Give the clay bead cap a gentle tap after every few rows to set in place.

35 When the bead cap reaches the middle of the bead, pull on the rope to break it. Roll the end into a point and tuck it in. Gently pat the rope so it adheres to the bead.

36 Cure for 45 minutes and then apply shoe polish to the bead with a firm paintbrush. Rub off the excess with a soft cloth or paper towel.

Multi-Direction Wrapped Bead

37 Extrude a long, narrow string of black polymer clay; set aside. Make a 20mm base bead from translucent clay. Poke a hole in the middle of the bead with a needle tool; keep the bead on the needle tool for the next step.

38 Wrap the long, narrow string of black polymer clay around the 20mm base bead, switching direction frequently and gently patting the string onto the base bead as you go **(Figure 9)**. Don't worry if the string breaks. Just tap down the end and start a new piece. Keep wrapping in different directions until you achieve an evenly random effect. Break off the end piece and tuck it next to another string so that it has a nicely finished appearance.

39 Cure for 45 minutes.

Disks

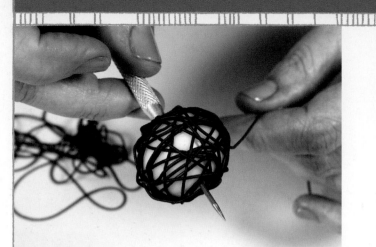

FIGURE 9

COLOR RECIPE

DISK MARBLE MIX:
1 part translucent polymer clay
½ part white polymer clay
⅛ part black polymer clay

40 Mix clay according to the Disk Marble Mix Color Recipe above.

41 Start with a 15mm round bead of clay made with the marble mix and then flatten it. (You will need larger beads for larger or wider disks, so it's a good idea to experiment with scrap clay to see what size disks you can make from the beads.) To give the disk its wavy shape, hold it in both hands between your thumb and forefinger and give a little twist so the disk is no longer flat but rather has an "undulating" form.

42 Poke a hole in the middle of the disk with a needle tool.

43 Repeat Steps 46–47 twenty-three times for a total of twenty-four disks of differing sizes from ½–1" (1.3–2.5 cm). Place disks on a piece of paper and cure for 40 minutes.

Wire Ball Bead

TIP

Rather than trying to estimate how much wire you'll need—this is an imprecise endeavor—work from a large coil of wire.

44 Begin by grasping the end of the wire with flat-nose or chain-nose pliers. Holding the coil of wire in your nondominant hand, use your dominant hand to curve it into a loose loop to start forming a ball of wire (**Figure 10**). Rather than waste wire and make the ball unnecessarily heavy, make the wrapped ball as loose as possible so the center is as hollow as possible (**Figure 11**). It may be easier to imagine that you're wrapping the wire around a ball of air. Wrap the wire in different directions to form a sphere.

45 Continue wrapping the wire, but when the ball is almost as big as you want, make the wraps tighter and closer together.

46 When the ball is the size you want, cut the end with flush cutters and bend the wire tail to tuck it inside the wire ball.

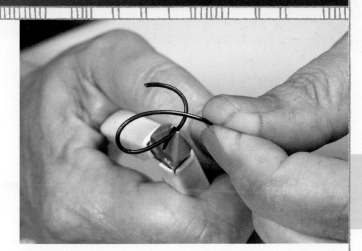

FIGURE 10

FIGURE 11

Zebra Cane Bead

Note: The steps below describe the process for making a zebra cane, which simply consists of stacking one color on top of another, cutting them in half and stacking again, repeating the process until they have the amount and thickness of stripes you want. Occasionally "squishing" the layers to achieve the distortion that occurs naturally in zebras.

47 Make a cork clay or aluminum foil 19mm base bead; set aside. Roll out black and translucent sheets of clay on the thickest setting of the pasta machine.

48 Place the sheets on top of each other to form two layers. Cut or tear the layered clay in half and then place one half on top of the other so that you have doubled the layers of alternating colors. Cut in half again and place one half on top of the other so you again double layers of alternating colors (**Figure 12**).

49 Pinch the stacked clay in a few places so the lines are no longer straight (**Figure 13**).

50 Cut that block in half and layer again and then repeat. Congratulations! You now have a zebra cane (**Figure 14**).

51 Cut slices from the side of the zebra cane and press them onto the base bead (**Figure 15**). Roll the slices into the surface of the bead by rolling the bead between your palms.

52 Poke a hole in the middle of the bead with a needle tool. Cure for 45 minutes.

53 Apply the shoe polish with a firm paintbrush and then rub off the excess with a soft cloth or paper towel.

Make the Clasp

54 Use the 14-gauge wire to make the Basic Clasp according to the instructions on p. 23. Modify if desired according to the suggestions on p. 23.

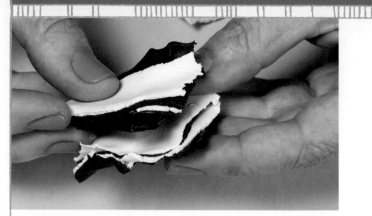

FIGURE 12

FIGURE 13

FIGURE 14

FIGURE 15

Assembling Necklace

55 Use the beading wire to string (p. 129) 1 crimp bead and 1 jump ring. Pass back through the crimp bead and flatten with flat- or chain-nose pliers. String 2 spacer beads, 4 Disks, 2 spacer beads, the Ring Bead, 2 spacer beads, 2 Disks, 2 spacer beads, the Zebra Cane Bead, 2 spacer beads, 2 Disks, 2 spacer beads, 1 Black Hemisphere Bead, 2 spacer beads, the Striped-Band Bead, 2 spacer beads, 2 Disks, 2 spacer beads, 1 Black-Hole Hemisphere Bead, 2 spacer beads, the translucent/white Circle-Embellished Bead, 2 spacer beads, 2 Disks, 2 spacer beads, the Wire Ball Bead, 2 spacer beads, 2 Disks, 2 spacer beads, the black/white/translucent Circle-Embellished Bead, 2 spacer beads, the other Black-Hole Hemisphere Bead, 2 spacer beads, 2 Disks, 2 spacer beads, the Cane-Banded Bead, 2 spacer beads, the other Black Half-Bead, 2 spacer beads, 2 Disks, 2 spacer beads, the Wrap-Capped Bead, 2 spacer beads, 2 Disks, 2 spacer beads, the Multi-Direction Wrapped Bead, 2 spacer beads, 4 Disks, 2 spacer beads, 1 crimp bead and 1 jump ring. Pass back through the crimp bead and flatten with flat- or chain-nose pliers. Pass the beading wire back through several beads and trim. String the clasp onto one of the jump rings.

To close the necklace, use the second jump ring as the ring half of the clasp.

MAMA'S MAMBO
{ BRACELET }

THIS BRACELET IS SO JOYOUS. THE WAVY SPACERS and rich jewel tones exude energy. The watercolor bead and the hemisphere bead serve as strong focal elements, each incorporating skinny polymer-clay strings from the extruder. The muted colors and even coils of the hemisphere bead stand in stark contrast to the colorful, undulating lines of the watercolor bead. The whole design is punctuated by the delightful irregularly shaped sterling silver spacer beads.

Finished Size: 9½" (24 cm) circumference

MATERIALS

Polymer clay in black, white, translucent, yellow, gold, red pearl, orange, turquoise, and blue

2 silver 8–10mm irregularly shaped embellishment/spacer beads

Brown shoe polish

About 12" (30.5 cm) of elastic beading cord

Cyanocrylate glue

TOOLS

Pasta machine or acrylic roller

Tissue blade

Needle tool

1¼" (3.2 cm) diameter decorative round light bulb to use as a mold

Extruder

Latex gloves (optional)

Firm paintbrush

bracelet

Disks

COLOR RECIPE

DISKS AND WATERCOLOR BEAD:
Using a pasta machine or an acrylic roller, combine yellow, gold, red pearl, orange, white, turquoise, blue, and translucent polymer clays in varying amounts to create marble mixes for a variety of Disks. For the Watercolor Bead, use the colors listed above and see Steps 10–14 on p. 59 for instructions.

1   Create a marble mix according to the Disks and Watercolor Bead Color Recipe above. Create 39 disks with the marble mix by rolling balls of clay in varying sizes (about 15–20 mm), then flattening them to create disks. The disks should range in size from ¾–1" (2–2.5 cm).

2   Pinch all around the edges to give the disks more interest and dimension. To give the disk its wavy shape, hold it in both hands between your thumb and forefinger and give a little twist so the disk is no longer flat but rather has an "undulating" form (**Figure 1**). Poke a hole in the middle of the disk with a needle tool.

3   Lay disks on flat paper and cure for 35 minutes (**Figure 2**).

Extruded-String Hemisphere Bead

COLOR RECIPE

EXTRUDED-STRING HEMISPHERE BEAD:
1 part gold polymer clay
1 part turquoise polymer clay
½ part white polymer clay
¼ part black polymer clay

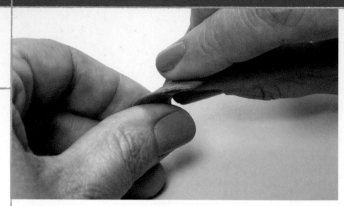

FIGURE 1

FIGURE 2

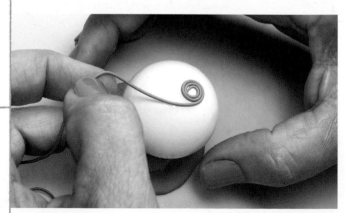

FIGURE 3

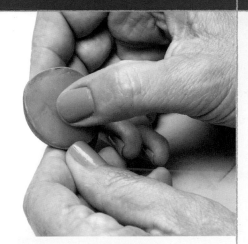

FIGURE 4

FIGURE 5

7 Cure for 15 minutes.

8 Fill the bead cap with translucent clay and smooth the surface with your fingers (**Figure 4**). Poke a hole in the middle of the hemisphere bead with a needle tool.

9 Cure for 45 minutes.

Watercolor Bead

10 Using the colors listed in the Disks and Watercolor Bead Color Recipe on p. 58, put little chunks of clay into the extruder to create a multicolor mix. Extrude a long string.

11 Make a 25mm base bead of translucent clay and then cover it randomly with the extruded strings (**Figure 5**).

12 Blend the extruded strings into the bead, using the same technique you use to roll a round bead. Because you are working with translucent clay (and a smooth bead will make a beautiful contrast to the organic disks), use latex gloves when you roll the bead to impart a smooth finish.

13 Poke a hole in the middle of the bead with a needle tool. Cure for 45 minutes.

14 Once the bead has cooled, apply the shoe polish with a firm paintbrush. Rub off the excess with a soft cloth or paper towel.

Assemble the bracelet

15 Use elastic beading cord to string the Watercolor Bead, 2 disks, 1 silver spacer, and the Extruded-String Hemisphere Bead. String (1 silver spacer and 1 disk) thirty-seven times. Tie a double overhand knot (p. 129) with the ends of the elastic. The elastic should end at the watercolor bead so you can hide the knot. Strengthen with a drop of cyanoacrylate glue inside the bead hole and tuck the knot inside by pushing it into the bead hole with the needle tool.

4 Mix clay according to the Extruded-String Hemi-sphere Bead Color Recipe on p. 58.

5 Extrude a long string from the extruder, using the smallest hole attachment.

6 Starting at the center, wind the string onto a light bulb to create a bead cap, leaving a small hole in the center (**Figure 3**).

MAMA'S MAMBO BRACELET

ARIA'S DREAM
{ NECKLACE }

THIS NECKLACE COMBINES PRIMITIVE STYLE WITH
BRIGHT COLORS—a fun combination. Shaping the beads over
cornstarch packing peanuts yields interesting organic shapes. The subtle marbling of the polymer clay, combined with the irregular shapes
of the beads, add to the visual intrigue, while the toggle clasp, leather
cord, and whimsical wire embellishments add to its charm.

Finished Size: 9½" (24 cm) circumference

MATERIALS

Polymer clay in black, white, translucent, orange, and zinc yellow

Liquid polymer clay

Cornstarch packing peanuts

20" (51 cm) of black 2mm leather
cord

6 large-holed black size 6° seed
beads

1' (30.5 cm) of oxidized sterling
silver 22-gauge wire

Ice water

Cyanoacrylate glue

TOOLS

Pasta machine or acrylic roller

½" (1.3 cm) thin acrylic roller

Tissue blade

Needle tool

Candelabra-base decorative vanity
globe light bulb to use as a mold

Bench block and bench block pad

Ball-peen hammer

necklace

Spiral Cane

1 Roll out a length of white clay on the medium setting of the pasta machine and cut a strip about 1" (2.5 cm) wide × 6" (15 cm) long.

2 Roll out a length of black clay on the medium setting of the pasta machine, then lay the white clay on top of the black clay. Cut the black clay down to the measurements of the white clay (**Figure 1**). Pat the pieces together.

3 Starting at a short end, roll the clay up (**Figure 2**) and seal the edge by pinching it.

4 Reduce the cane (clay just rolled) by gently turning and pinching it along the length so it gets longer and narrower. Set aside.

FIGURE 1

FIGURE 2

FIGURE 3

FIGURE 4

FIGURE 5

FIGURE 6

FIGURE 7

Simple Lace Cane

5 Roll a 3" (7.5 cm) log of white clay (**Figure 3**).

6 Roll a length of black clay wide enough to cover the white log.

7 Cut one edge of the black clay so you have a straight edge. Place the white log onto the black clay next to the straight edge (**Figure 4**) and begin to roll up the black clay over the white log.

8 Continue rolling until the edge of black clay meets the rest of the sheet of black clay. Unroll it slightly, and you will see a mark where the edge of the clay has hit the sheet of clay. Cut a straight line there with a tissue blade (**Figure 5**).

9 Seal the edge by pinching it together (**Figure 6**).

10 Reduce the cane by gently turning and pinching it so it gets longer and narrower.

11 Cut the cane into two lengths and place them side by side. Nudge them together so the circles become oblong ovals (**Figure 7**).

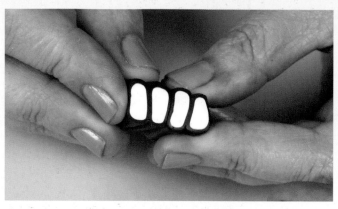

FIGURE 8

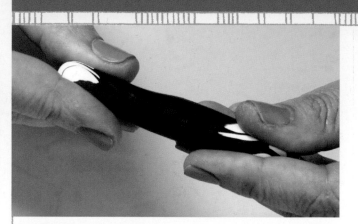

FIGURE 9

12 Cut the new double-thickness cane into two lengths and place them together again as before. Nudge them together again, squishing them slightly so the ovals are very skinny and all running in the same direction (**Figure 8**).

13 Reduce the cane by gently turning and pinching it so it gets longer and narrower (**Figure 9**). Set aside.

Complex Lace Cane

14 Cut the simple lace cane (created in Steps 5–13) in half and combine the two halves but do not line them up evenly. One of the pieces should be at a bit of an angle to the other (**Figure 10**).

15 Reduce the cane by turning and pinching it as before, then cut in half and combine again, once again not lined up evenly (**Figure 11**).

16 Repeat Step 15.

17 Roll out a sheet of black clay on a thin setting of the pasta machine and cover the cane just made with the sheet (**Figure 12**). Set aside.

FIGURE 10

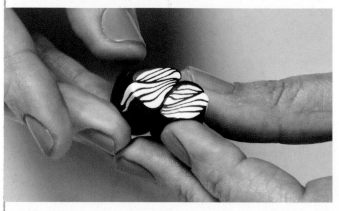

FIGURE 11

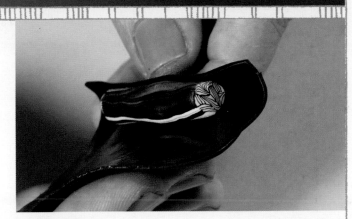

FIGURE 12

FIGURE 13

FIGURE 14

Stripe-Banded Bead

18 Make a 13mm black base bead out of solid black polymer clay; set aside.

19 Roll a rope made from small pieces of black and white polymer clay and wrap the rope around the middle of the solid black base bead (**Figure 13**).

20 Gently pat the rope down so it stays put and then roll it more firmly so it is smoothly blended into the black clay. The effect will be a striped band. Use rubber gloves to achieve a smooth surface (**Figure 14**).

21 Poke a hole through the bead with a needle tool and cure for 45 minutes.

Lumpy Hollow Beads

COLOR RECIPE

LUMPY HOLLOW BEAD MARBLE MIX:
1½ parts orange polymer clay
1 part gold polymer clay
1 part translucent polymer clay
½ part zinc yellow polymer clay
½ part white polymer clay

22 Mix a subtle marble mix, according to the Lumpy Hollow Bead Marble Blend Color Recipe Mix above, that will be the background color of the beads. Roll the marble into a sheet, using a thick setting on the pasta machine.

23 Squish two packing peanuts together to form a lumpy ball. You can add a drop of water to act as a glue to keep them together.

24 Cover the packing-peanut ball with the marbled polymer clay sheet. Roll it in your hand like you're rolling a ball. It will be lumpy since the packing-peanut core is lumpy.

25 Embellish with thin slices from the Spiral, Simple Lace, and Complex Lace Canes (created in Steps 1–17). If the slices are thin, it's easier to blend them into the base bead clay. Because you are working on

ARIA'S DREAM NECKLACE

such a small scale, you may find it easier to use a ½"
(1.3 cm) thin acrylic roller to completely blend the
cane slices into the bead (**Figure 15**).

26 Poke a large hole through the bead with a wooden
skewer (or other poking tool that is fatter than a
needle tool) and cure for 30 minutes.

27 After the bead is cool, submerge it in water to dissolve the cornstarch core. You don't have to dissolve
the cornstarch—it is so light it doesn't add much
weight to the bead but it can be difficult to thread
wire or cord through it. Once the cornstarch is saturated with water it will start to dissolve. The easiest
and quickest way to get all of it out is simply to put
your mouth over one hole and blow the cornstarch
out through the other. You may need to dunk and
blow a few times to get all of the cornstarch out.

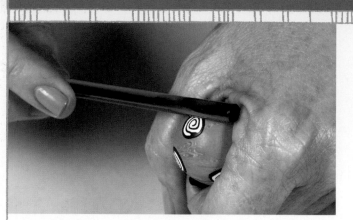

FIGURE 15

Bead Caps

28 Form a bead cap over a light bulb mold with orange
clay and embellish with thin slices of Spiral, Simple
Lace, and Complex Lace Canes (created in Steps
1–17) as desired (as in Step 26). Poke a hole large
enough to accommodate leather cord in the middle of
the bead cap with a needle tool. Cure for 15 minutes.

Button Toggle Clasp

29 Make a large spiral by slicing a very thick slice from
the Spiral Cane and then flattening it. You will get a
large spiral that you can use to embellish the button
clasp (**Figure 16**).

FIGURE 16

30 Form a bead cap over a light bulb mold with orange
clay and embellish with the large spiral just made
(**Figure 17**). Cure for 15 minutes.

31 Tie a knot at the end of a 24" (61 cm) length of
leather cord.

Place the knotted end of the cord into the bead cap,
add a few drops of liquid polymer clay, and fill the
bead cap up with black polymer clay, covering and

FIGURE 17

FIGURE 18

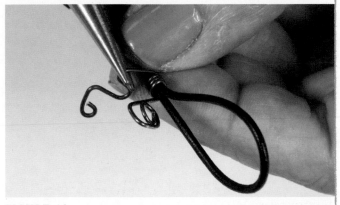

FIGURE 19

FIGURE 20

hiding the knot. Be sure to apply the clay so that the leather cord sticks straight out of the middle of the bead cap. Pinch the clay from the edges and smooth the surface and edges with your fingers (Figure 18). Cure for 40 minutes, put into ice water for a few minutes, then dry off.

Assembly

32   String (p. 129) 1 seed bead, (1 Lumpy Hollow Bead and 1 seed bead) twice, 1 Bead Cap, the Stripe-Banded Bead, 1 Bead Cap, (1 seed bead and 1 Lumpy Hollow Bead) twice, and 1 seed bead onto the leather cord.

33   Create a loop for the toggle clasp, making sure the leather cord slips snugly but easily over the button toggle clasp. Leaving a tail of a few inches of wire, bind the loop tightly by coiling with 22-gauge wire. Leave another tail a few inches long and trim the wire.

34   Bend one of the ends of wire into a loose spiral and make several half loops in opposite directions with the other end (Figure 19).

35   After bending the ends of the wire to form the embellishment, bend them upward temporarily to fit onto the bench block and pound them with a ball-peen hammer to texture and flatten (Figure 20). After pounding them, you can bend them back against the leather cord.

36   Affix the focal bead to the leather cord with a drop of cyanoacrylate glue so it stays at the bottom of the neck-lace and the clasp stays put at the back of the neck.

VARIATION IDEA

The toggle clasp and wire detail for the leather loop on this necklace are very intriguing. Consider designing a necklace where they serve as the focal element instead, so you have a simple lightweight lariat design—just the toggle and embellished loop on a length of leather or hand-dyed silk cord. Fun!

ARIA'S DREAM NECKLACE

LUSH SONATA
{ NECKLACE }

PART OF THE CHARM OF THIS NECKLACE is the contrast of the zebra beads with the peach marbling of the bead caps. The unexpected juxtaposition of elements creates just a touch of sophisticated whimsy, while the remarkably spare design of the cable neck ring serves as a simple backdrop for the luscious beads.

Finished Size: 17½" (44.5 cm) circumference

MATERIALS

Polymer clay in black, white, translucent, orange, gold, and crimson

Liquid polymer clay

2 cork clay or aluminum foil 25mm base beads

12' (3.6 m) of black 19-gauge steel wire for wire-ball bead

16–18" (40.5–45.5 cm) sterling silver tension-clasp neck cable

2 black 6mm accent beads

Ice water

Cyanoacrylate glue

TOOLS

Pasta machine or acrylic roller

Tissue blade

Needle tool

Standard-size light bulbs to use as molds

Flat-nose or chain-nose pliers

Round-nose pliers

Flush cutters

Ball-peen hammer

Bench block and bench block cushion

Latex gloves (optional)

necklace

Bead Caps

COLOR RECIPE

BEAD CAP MARBLE MIX:
1 part orange polymer clay
1 part translucent polymer clay
½ part gold polymer clay
¼ part white polymer clay
¼ part crimson polymer clay

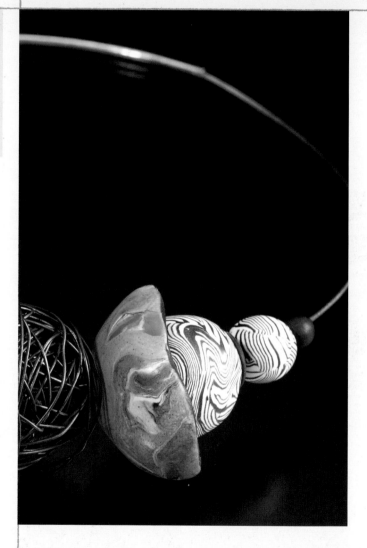

1   Mix clay according to the Bead Cap Marble Mix Color Recipe above. Divide it in half.

2   Using a light bulb as a mold, form a circle of clay onto the bulb (this will become a bead cap). If you want the bead cap to be smooth, wear latex gloves to smooth the surface. Poke a hole in the middle of the bead cap with a needle tool. Cure for 15 minutes; allow to cool.

3   Roll out a thin sheet of black clay, large enough to cover the inside of the bead cap. Spread a few drops of liquid polymer clay over the inside of the cap, drape the thin sheet of clay over the inside of the bead cap and press it onto the surface. Use your fingers to pull off the extra clay from the edges.

4   Pat the clay onto the surface and blend it to the edge of the rim so it adheres to the bead cap. Poke a hole through the first hole in the middle of the bead cap with a needle tool.

5   Repeat Steps 1–4 to create a second Bead Cap. Cure both caps for 25 minutes. After the Bead Cap has been removed from the light bulb, place it into ice water for a few minutes. Dry the Bead Cap and set aside.

FIGURE 1

FIGURE 4

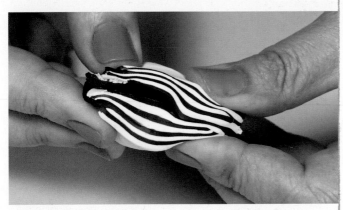

FIGURE 2

FIGURE 3

Zebra Cane Beads

Note: The steps below describe the process for making a zebra cane, which simply consists of stacking one color on top of another, cutting them in half and stacking again, repeating the process until they have the amount and thickness of stripes you want, and occasionally "squishing" the layers to achieve the distortion that occurs naturally in zebras.

6   Roll out black and white sheets of clay on the thickest setting of the pasta machine.

7   Place the sheets on top of each other to form two layers. Cut the layered clay in half and then place one half on top of the other so that you have doubled the layers of alternating colors. Cut in half again and place one half on top of the other so you again double layers of alternating colors (**Figure 1**).

8   Pinch the stacked clay in a few places so the lines are no longer straight (**Figure 2**).

9   Cut that block in half and layer again and then repeat. Congratulations! You now have a zebra cane (**Figure 3**).

10   To form the larger beads, cut slices from the side of the zebra cane and press them onto the two 25mm base beads. To form the smaller beads, make two 13mm base beads from scrap clay, then press slices from the cane over these base beads (**Figure 4**). Roll the slices into the surface of the bead by rolling the bead between your palms.

LUSH SONATA NECKLACE

11 Poke a hole in the middle of the bead cap with a needle tool. Cure for 45 minutes.

12 Form small black bead caps for the larger zebra beads by forming round 10mm beads out of black clay and then pressing them onto the ends of the zebra beads. They will flatten out, forming bead caps. Cure for 20 minutes.

Wire-Ball Bead

TIP

Rather than trying to estimate how much wire you'll need—this is an imprecise endeavor—work from a large coil of wire.

13 Begin by grasping the end of the 19-gauge wire with flat- or chain-nose pliers. Holding the coil of wire in your nondominant hand, curve it to start forming a ball of wire **(Figure 5)**. Rather than waste wire and make the ball unnecessarily heavy, make the wrapped ball as loose as possible so the center is as hollow as possible **(Figure 6)**. It may be easier to imagine that you're wrapping the wire around a ball of air. Wrap the wire in different directions to form a sphere.

14 Continue wrapping the wire, but when the ball is almost as big as you want it to be, make the wraps tighter and closer together **(Figure 7)**.

15 When the ball reaches the desired size, use flush cutters to trim the end and bend the wire tail to tuck it inside the wire ball.

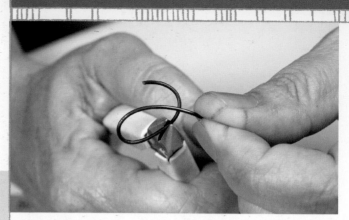

FIGURE 5

FIGURE 6

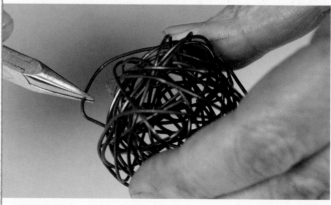

FIGURE 7

Assemble Necklace

16 String (p. 129) the necklace onto the neck cable in the following order: 1 small black accent bead, 1 small Zebra Cane bead, 1 small black Bead Cap (from outside to inside), 1 large Zebra Cane bead, 1 marbled Bead Cap (from inside to outside), the Wire-Ball bead, 1 marbled Bead Cap (from outside to inside), 1 large Zebra Cane bead, 1 small black Bead Cap (from inside to outside), 1 small Zebra Cane bead, and 1 small black accent bead.

17 To prevent the clasp from slipping down when wearing the necklace, put a few drops of cyanoacrylate glue inside the bead holes of two beads and allow to dry so that the beads adhere to the cable (be sure they are placed where you want them to stay permanently).

DESERT ABUNDANCE
{ BRACELET }

REMINISCENT OF A HAWAIIAN LEI, THIS PIECE engages the eye on several levels as the color palette moves from purple to teal. The primitive bone spacer beads add to the organic effect, and the addition of the warm tones and interesting texture of the cogged brass heishi add complexity to its charm. Because these disks are so thin, this bracelet weighs almost nothing.

Finished Size: 9" (23 cm) circumference

MATERIALS

Polymer clay in white, translucent, turquoise, gold, and purple

44 shell or bone 4–6mm spacer beads

92 cogged brass 3mm heishi spacer beads

12" (30.5 cm) of elastic beading cord

Cyanoacrylate glue

Fiberfill cut to fit into convection oven

TOOLS

Pasta machine or acrylic roller

Needle tool

Extruder

Scissors

bracelet

Disks

COLOR RECIPES

DISKS AND FOCAL BEAD:

COLOR 1

1 part turquoise polymer clay

½ part white polymer clay

½ part gold polymer clay

COLOR 2

1 part turquoise polymer clay

1 part white polymer clay

½ part gold polymer clay

COLOR 3

1 part purple polymer clay

1 part translucent polymer clay

½ part turquoise polymer clay

½ part white polymer clay

COLOR 4

1 part turquoise polymer clay

1 part translucent polymer clay

1 part white polymer clay

½ part purple polymer clay

1   Mix four different batches of color according to the Color Recipes for the Disks and Focal Bead at left, leaving the batches slightly marbled.

2   Roll 21 round beads (or desired number), each about 10mm in size. Make several of each color mixed in Step 1; vary them slightly in size and shape. It's a good idea to make a few more than you think you need so you have the luxury of discarding a few or using fewer metal or bone spacers when you are assembling the bracelet.

3   Run the beads through the pasta machine at a medium setting so they are uniformly flat.

4   Lay the disks on paper. Poke holes with a needle tool while the disks are laying flat on the paper and cure for 25 minutes.

Pod Focal Bead

5   Form a pod shape onto a needle tool by putting a 19mm ball of translucent clay onto the shaft of the needle tool and pinching at each end to narrow and elongate the ends (**Figure 1**).

6   Extrude narrow strings of clay, using one of the colors mixed in Step 1 and gently lay them onto the pod shape. As you're working, tap them down so they stick to the pod. Since the strings are so narrow, it's easy to break them—don't worry! This just adds to the visual interest (**Figure 2**). Continue laying down the extruded strings until the pod is completely covered. Break the strings off near the edge of the bead and be sure that the bead hole is left free of obstruction.

7   Cure on fiberfill (or make a paper fan if you prefer) for 45 minutes.

FIGURE 1

FIGURE 2

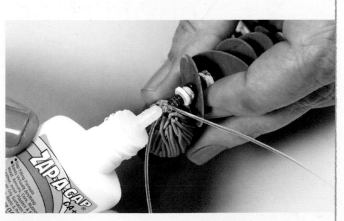

FIGURE 3

Assembly

8 String (p. 129) the bracelet onto the elastic cord in the following order, keeping like-colored Disks together for an ombre effect: 4 metal spacer beads, 2 bone spacer beads, 2 metal spacer beads, (1 Disk, 2 metal spacer beads, 2 bone spacer beads, 2 metal spacer beads) 20 times, 2 metal spacer beads, 2 bone spacer beads, 4 metal spacer beads and the Pod Focal Bead.

9 Tie the ends of the elastic cord with a double overhand knot (p. 129), then hide the knot inside the hole of the Pod Focal Bead by tucking it into the hole with a needle tool. Put a drop of cyanoacrylate glue as close to the inside of the bead hole as you can get it so the knot stays put (**Figure 3**). Trim the ends of the elastic cord.

VARIATION IDEA

This bracelet also makes a delightful necklace. Simply increase the length of the elastic cord and the number of disks and spacer beads. This also gives you more room to play with, so you can include more disk colors.

SPRINGTIME AFTERNOON
{ BRACELET }

IF THIS WERE A COOKBOOK, THIS PROJECT WOULD BE a "quick and easy" recipe, but don't be fooled. This little bracelet still packs maximum effect. The combination of the dark wire with delicate petal-thin polymer clay disks creates a uniquely pleasing design. Pink definitely takes a walk on the wilder side in this creation.

Finished Size: 7½" (19 cm) circumference

MATERIALS

Polymer clay in black, white, translucent, fuchsia, and gold

Liquid polymer clay

Pink metallic powder

22' (6.7 m) of black 19-gauge steel wire

12" (30.5 cm) of elastic beading cord

Cyanoacrylate glue

TOOLS

Pasta machine or acrylic roller

Tissue blade

Needle tool

Extruder

Wooden skewer or small wooden dowel

Flat- or chain-nose pliers

Flush cutters

Latex gloves (optional)

Soft paintbrush

Dust mask

bracelet

Wrapped-Cap Bead

1   Make a marble mix according to the Wrapped-Cap Bead Marble Mix Color Recipe above.

2   Roll a 19mm round bead from the marble mix. If you want it to be smooth and free of fingerprints, wear latex gloves for the final rolling.

3   Poke a hole through the bead with the needle tool.

4   Extrude a long, narrow string of black polymer clay.

5   Holding your bead perched on the needle tool, spread a drop or two of liquid polymer clay onto the bead, near the top bead hole. Lay the end of the extruded string flush against (but not on top of) the hole and tap it down so it stays put (this is the point from which you will begin to form the wrapped cap; **Figure 1**).

6   Carefully turn the bead and let gravity help the string wrap itself around the tip of the bead, forming a wrapped cap. Give the wrapped-cap strands a gentle tap after every few rows to set them in place.

7   When the bead cap is about 15mm long, break the strand off. Use your thumb and forefinger to roll the end of the strand into a point and tuck it into the previous wraps. Gently pat the end of the strand so it adheres to the bead.

8   Turn the bead over and repeat Steps 5–8 so you have matching wrapped caps on each end.

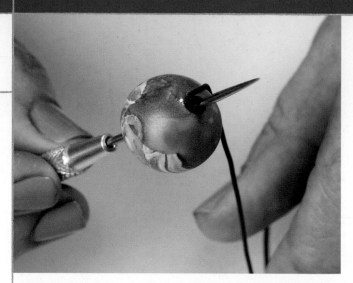

FIGURE 1

FIGURE 2

FIGURE 3

FIGURE 4

9 Wearing a protective dust mask, brush the caps with a very light dusting of metallic powder using a soft paintbrush **(Figure 2)**.

10 Cure for 45 minutes.

Disks

11 Make a simple cane by rolling the leftover marble mix from Step 1 into a log about 2" (5 cm) long × 1" (2.5 cm) wide.

12 Roll black clay into a very thin sheet with the pasta machine or acrylic roller. Use the clay sheet to cover the short marble-mix log **(Figure 3)**.

13 Reduce the cane by pinching and turning it until it is the diameter you want for the disks (about 15mm).

14 Slice 15 disks from the cane using the tissue blade **(Figure 4)**.

15 Run the disks through a medium setting of the pasta machine or roll them flat with the acrylic roller so they are all evenly flat.

16 Lay the disks on a flat surface, such as a piece of paper, and poke holes with a needle tool. Cure for 30 minutes.

Coiled-Tube Beads

17 Coil wire around a wooden skewer or small wooden dowel, but don't coil tightly; leave spaces between the coils so they have a "looser" look **(Figure 5)**.

18 When the coil is the desired length (about ½" [1.3 cm]), coil the wire back in the other direction, over the previous coils. Continue to coil loosely back and forth so the coils are uneven, imparting a primitive effect. When the tube beads have achieved the diameter you want, cut the end of the wire with flush cutters and tuck it into the bead so you don't have a loose wire end. Slide the bead off the wooden skewer.

19 Repeat Steps 17 and 18 thirteen times for a total of fourteen Coiled-Tube Beads.

Assembly

20 Using elastic beading cord, string (p. 129) the bracelet as follows: (1 Disk and 1 Coiled Tube Bead) 14 times, 1 Disk, and the Wrapped-Cap Bead. Tie the ends of the elastic cord together with a double overhand knot (p. 129), then apply a drop of cyanoacrylate glue to the knot and tuck it inside the hole of the Wrapped-Cap Bead. If your bottle of cyanoacrylate glue doesn't have a special long, narrow nozzle for detail work, you can put a dot of glue at the end of a wooden toothpick and dab the glue onto the knot, then immediately tuck the knot into the hole of the bead.

VARIATION IDEA

Try using a spiral cane (see p. 62) to form the disks. Combined with the Coiled-Tube Beads, the overall sensation will be one of movement and energy. You could also experiment with making disks from a variety of different types of canes for differing visual effects.

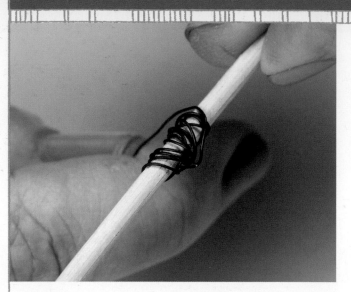

FIGURE 5

CIRCUS GALLERY Disks play a prominent role in this colorful bangle, but their thick undulating shapes and colorful edges provide a compelling alternative to Springtime Afternoon's thin bordered disks.

DANCING BELLS
{ EARRINGS }

THE INSPIRATION FOR THIS DESIGN CAME FROM a desire to create earrings that evoke the first springtime blooms of the season. The bells are reminiscent of flower petals and the wire dangles evoke stamens. I call them Dancing Bells because they move along with the wearer. Wearing them is as delightful and provocative as wearing a flower in your hair.

Finished Size: 7½" (19 cm) circumference

MATERIALS

Polymer clay in white, translucent, orange, crimson, and yellow

2' (61 cm) of sterling silver 20-gauge wire

4 sterling silver 5–6mm irregularly shaped spacer beads

Ice water

TOOLS

Pasta machine or acrylic roller

Round-nose pliers

2 pairs of chain- or flat-nose pliers

Flush cutters

Bench block and ball-peen hammer

File or wire rounder

Bent-tip candelabra-base light bulb to use as a mold

Liver of sulfur

#0000 steel wool

Soft polishing cloth

earrings

Polymer Clay Bells

COLOR RECIPE

POLYMER CLAY BELLS
1 part translucent polymer clay
½ part white polymer clay
½ part orange polymer clay
½ part crimson polymer clay
½ part yellow polymer clay

FIGURE 1

1   Make a marble blend, according to the Polymer Clay Bells Color Recipe above. Using chandelier light bulbs as a mold, form the marbled clay over the tips of the light bulbs by patting it onto the light bulb, until you have the desired "bell" shape (**Figure 1**). Make the walls thin so the earrings are lightweight and therefore comfortable to wear.

2   Cure the bells for 20 minutes. Since the walls of the polymer clay bells are thin, dip them in ice water before removing them from the light bulb. This will strengthen them to avoid tearing.

3   Form two small beads of translucent polymer clay, large enough to cover the top of the polymer clay bells. Place one on top of each bell.

4   Push the silver accent beads into the translucent polymer clay beads (placed on top of the bells (**Figure 2**). Cure for 30 minutes.

FIGURE 2

Dangles

5   Make dangles by using flush cutters to cut two pieces of 20-gauge wire, each about 2" (5 cm) long. Cut two more pieces, each about 2¼" (5.5 cm) long, and two more pieces, each about 2½" (6.5 cm) long. You now have six pieces of wire in three different sizes.

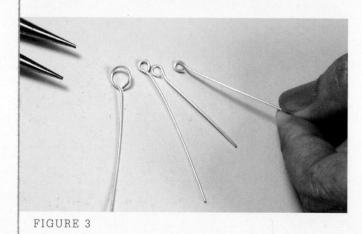

FIGURE 3

FIGURE 4

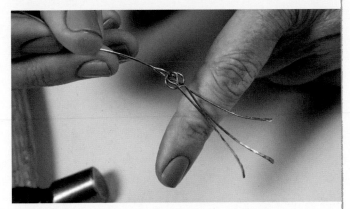

FIGURE 5

FIGURE 6

6 Form a small simple loop (p. 129) at one end of each of the pieces of wire. You now have dangles (**Figure 3**).

7 Place the dangles on a bench block and texture them with a ball-peen hammer. Flatten the straight ends of the wire dangles so they flare slightly and file them to eliminate any sharp points (**Figure 4**).

Ear Wires

8 Using flush cutters, cut two 4" (10 cm) lengths of 20-gauge wire. Form a small simple loop on one end of each 4" (10 cm) piece of wire (these will become your ear wires).

9 Open the simple loop of one of the 4" (10 cm) pieces of wire, as you would a jump ring (p. 129), and string the loops of 3 of the dangles, using one of each length (**Figure 5**). Repeat the entire step to string the remaining dangles onto the remaining 4" (10 cm) wire.

10 Antique the wires and dangles (now attached to each other) with liver of sulfur (p. 19).

11 Thread the straight end of the 4" (10 cm) wires up through the polymer clay bells.

12 Starting where the wire meets the accent bead, texture ¾" (2 cm) of the 4" (10 cm) wire by firmly squeezing round-nose pliers onto the wire. This adds interesting detail, and using round-nose pliers as a texturing tool flattens the wire so the beads are held in place.

13 Using the fattest part of the round-nose pliers, bend the wire above the textured portion over the pliers to form into the shape of an ear wire (**Figure 6**).

14 Trim the wire, leaving 1" (2.5 cm) tails of wire below the loop. File the ends of the ear wire tails with a file or wire rounder.

DANCING BELLS EARRINGS

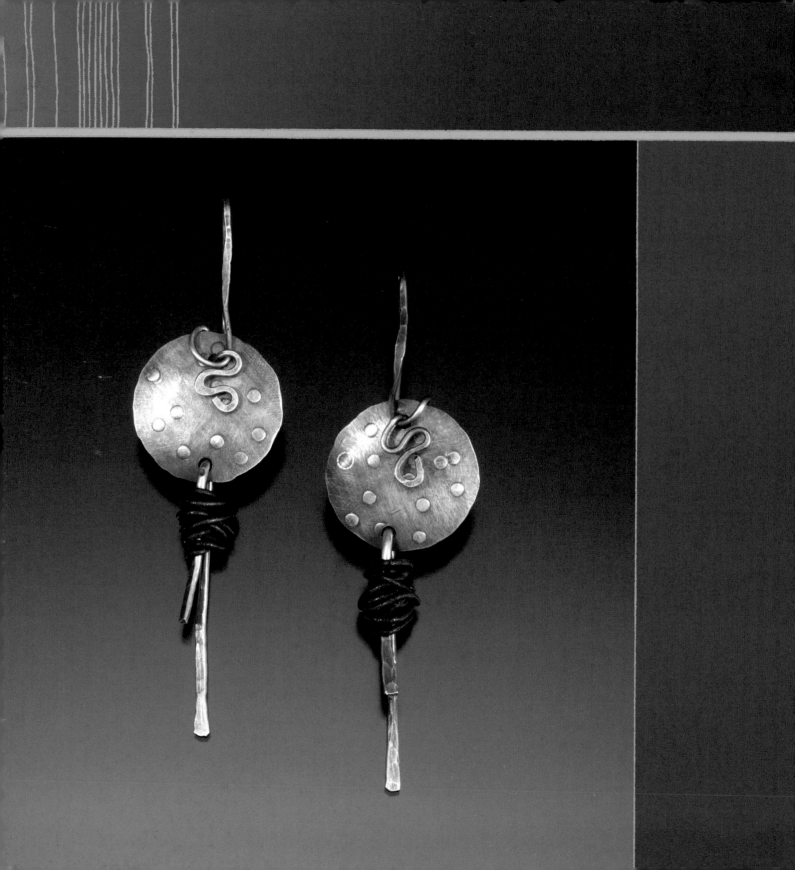

ZEN
{ EARRINGS }

**THE RANDOM PLACEMENT OF CIRCLES ON THESE
STERLING SILVER DISKS** reminds me of stars in the nighttime
sky. Although these earrings have been designed with circles embellishing the disks, you can also drill small holes in the disks for a different look that would still be reminiscent of that starry sky. The extruded polymer clay strings on the dangles have an intriguing fiber-like effect.

Finished Size: 2¾" (7 cm) long (including ear wires)

MATERIALS

Black polymer clay

Metallic powder

2½" (6.5 cm) sterling silver
24-gauge disks

12" (30.5 cm) of sterling silver
20-gauge wire for ear wires

8" (40.5 cm) of sterling silver
16-gauge wire for dangles

TOOLS

Extruder

Brush for metallic powder

Dust mask

Dapping punch or ball-peen
hammer

Dapping block (optional)

Texturing hammer (optional)

Bench block and bench block
cushion

Permanent marker

Two-hole metal punch

Round-nose pliers

Chain-nose pliers

Flush cutters

File or wire rounder

Liver of sulfur

#0000 steel wool

Soft paintbrush

Soft polishing cloth

earrings

Silver Disks

1 Texture the silver disks by laying them on the bench block and hitting them all over with a texturing or ball-peen hammer. Be sure to pound the edges well so you achieve an organic, textured edge **(Figure 1)**.

2 The disks can be left flat, but if you wish to dome them, gently dome them in a dapping die so you don't pound out the texturing. To dome a disk, place it into the round depression of a dapping die and gently pound it with a dapping punch or the round side of a ball-peen hammer until it takes the shape of the dome **(Figure 2)**.

3 Using the two-hole metal punch or a drill, make a hole close to the edge of the disk **(Figure 3)** and then a second hole, close to the edge on the opposite side of the disk, directly across from the first hole. You may find it helpful to make marks for the holes with a permanent marker so you'll know where to place the hole punch.

4 If you have never used a two-hole punch before, it would be a good idea to practice on a piece of scrap metal first. Form random raised dots with the two-hole punch by using the same technique you'd use to punch a hole; turn the screw mechanism but don't apply enough pressure to push all the way through. Once you feel the mandrel of the two-hole punch touch the disk, just turn it ever-so-slightly farther, and you'll get delightful circles. If you would like to achieve indentations rather than raised dots, hold the disk convex-side up as you form them.

FIGURE 1

FIGURE 2

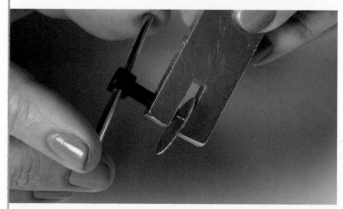

FIGURE 3

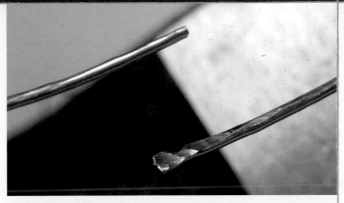

FIGURE 4

FIGURE 5

FIGURE 6

Wire Dangles

5 Cut two 4" (10 cm) pieces of 16-gauge wire. Texture the wire by laying it on the bench block and pounding with a texturing hammer but be sure not to flatten it so much that you can no longer fit it through the hole in the disk (**Figure 4**).

6 Feed one wire through one of the holes on one disk and bend it in half, but not exactly at the midpoint, so that the wires hang down from the disk; your earrings will be more attractive if the two ends are not exactly the same length. Flatten the ends of the wire more so that they flare out. File the ends to smooth out any rough or sharp edges. Repeat entire step with the remaining wire and disk.

Ear Wires

7 Cut two 4" (10 cm) pieces of 20-gauge wire. Make an embellishment near the end of one wire by forming three small loops in alternating directions with round-nose pliers. Repeat to embellish second wire (**Figure 5**).

8 Pound the looped portions of the wires to texture and flatten them.

9 Thread one wire through the hole at the top of one disk from front (convex side) to back (concave side), then loop the tail of wire back over to the front of the disk. Bend the wire and anchor it under the embellishment, then bend it straight up from the disk.

10 Flatten and texture 1" (2.5 cm) of the remaining wire. Using the fattest part of the round-nose pliers, bend the wire above the textured portion over the pliers to form into the shape of an ear wire (**Figure 6**).

11 Repeat Steps 9 and 10 for a second ear wire on the second disk but remember to make the embellishments mirror images of each other instead of identical. You may need to trim the ear wire ends so they are equal length. Be sure to leave 1" (2.5 cm) tails of wire below the curve of the ear wire. File the ends of the ear wire tails with a file or wire rounder.

ZEN EARRINGS

12 Antique the earrings with liver of sulfur (p. 19) and polish with #0000 steel wool. If you gently rub the steel wool in different directions on the disk, you can enhance the design with the fine scratches of the steel wool. The straight lines from the steel fiber scratches are an interesting and pleasing contrast to the round circles. Finish off with a soft polishing cloth.

Polymer Clay Embellishment

13 Extrude a long, thin string of black polymer clay.

14 Wrap a polymer clay string around the wire dangles on each earring **(Figure 7)**. When you are happy with the size and shape of the wrap, lightly squeeze and roll the end of each of the polymer strings to make them thinner, then tuck the ends into the wraps so they don't show.

15 Lightly press the clay to secure it to the wraps.

16 Wearing a protective dust mask, dust the clay wraps with metallic powder using a paintbrush **(Figure 8)**.

17 Cure for 30 minutes.

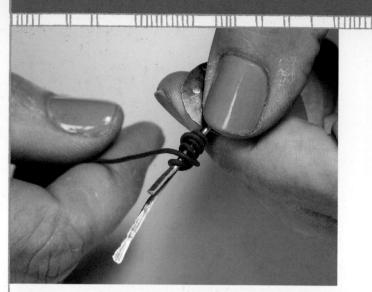

FIGURE 7

FIGURE 8

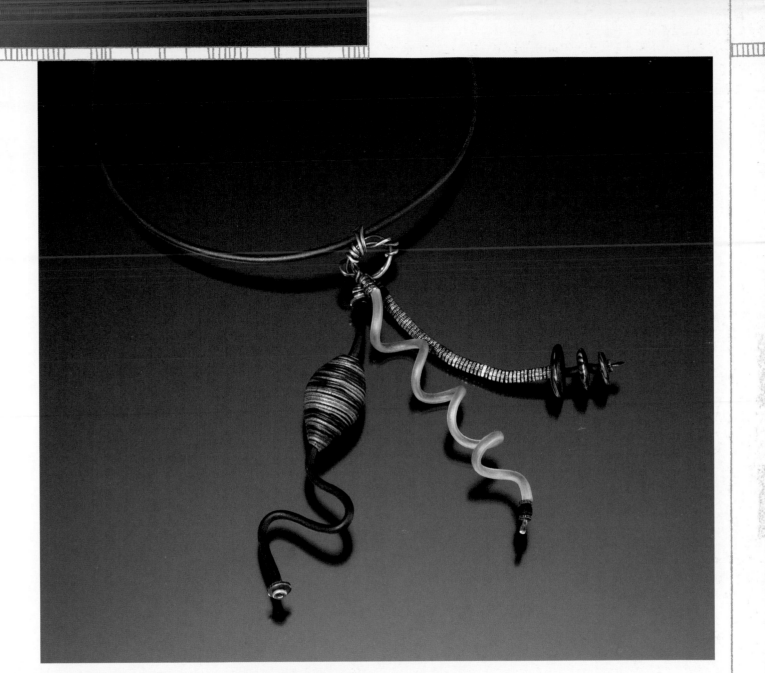

MAINLAND EUPHORIA Extruded polymer clay string takes
on a completely different look when several colors of clay are
extruded and then evenly wound around a base bead. Dangles
form the focal element in this necklace but could also be used to
design elegant but quirky earrings.

TWICE TOLD STORY
{ RING }

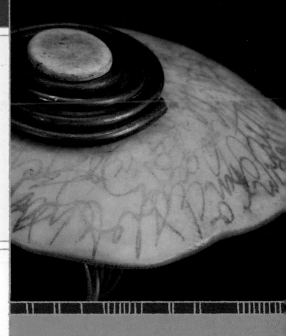

JEWELRY THAT INCORPORATES WORDS or even the hint of words is always particularly evocative. Whose story does it tell? That of the artist or that of the wearer? Or both? Writing and drawing on the clay can add depth to your understanding of working with polymer clay and inspire new ideas for jewelry and art.

Finished Size (of polymer clay top): 1½ × 1¾" (3.8 × 4.5 cm)

MATERIALS

Polymer clay in black, white, translucent, gold, and turquoise

Liquid polymer clay

Brown shoe polish

30" (76 cm) of sterling silver or copper 16-gauge wire

Paper towel or extremely fine-grain wet/dry sandpaper

Ice water

TOOLS

Pasta machine or acrylic roller

3 × 3" (7.5 × 7.5 cm) Lucite square

Super-fine-point permanent marker

Ring mandrel or wooden dowel

Standard-size light bulb to use as a mold

Linoleum cutter

Chain-nose pliers

Flush cutters

Firm paintbrush

Liver of sulfur

#0000 steel wool

Soft polishing cloth

ring

TIP

Using a ring mandrel to form the shank helps you size the ring correctly, but since a ring mandrel is angled, it's tricky to make all the coils the same size. You may want to size it using a ring mandrel for the first wrap, then finish making the wraps around a wooden dowel to keep them even.

Clay Cap

COLOR RECIPE

CLAY CAP:
1 part translucent polymer clay
¼ part white polymer clay

FIGURE 1

1   Roll a 25–30mm ball, according to the Clay Cap Color Recipe above. Pinch the ball into a triangular shape and then run it through the pasta machine at a medium-thick setting or flatten it with an acrylic roller. If you aren't pleased with the shape, repeat the process of pinching a ball into a triangle and rolling it through again until you are happy with it and then place it onto a lightbulb to form a gently curved cap shape (**Figure 1**).

2   Cure the cap for 25 minutes. Dip it into a bowl of ice water for a few minutes to make it harder and more translucent.

3   Practice this step on scratch paper first! Using a super-fine-point permanent marker, write all over the cap. You can form legible words if you wish, but I prefer writing in a very loose way that evokes but doesn't quite depict words. I like to start at the middle and then work to the edge, but you may prefer to begin at the edge. I find it easiest to turn the cap as I'm working (**Figure 2**).

FIGURE 2

FIGURE 3

4   You may want to keep the writing dark, but if you want to achieve an ancient look, gently lay a paper towel over the ink before it is completely dry. Don't move the paper towel or you will smear the ink; just lay it down and gently pat it without moving or sliding it. You can also achieve a faded look by gently sanding with your finest-grain wet/dry sandpaper.

5   If you make a mistake, don't worry. You can just keep sanding until the ink disappears completely and then start over.

6   After the ink is completely dry, apply the brown shoe polish to the cap using a firm paintbrush. Rub off excess shoe polish with a soft cloth or paper towel.

7   Using a linoleum cutter, cut a small hole into the middle of the cap.

Ring Shank

8   Working from a coil of 16-gauge wire, leave a tail of about 4" (10 cm) and wrap wire four times around a ring mandrel or wooden dowel. You will be looping some wire directly above this coiled shank, which will make it fit tighter, so be sure to size it a little larger than the desired finished size **(Figure 3)**.

9   Cut the wire, leaving a tail of 8" (20.5 cm). Bend this tail so it sticks straight up from the ring shank. Coil the 4" (10 cm) tail of wire around the base of the 8" (20.5 cm) tail, trim the end of the 4" (10 cm) wire and tuck it into the coil **(Figure 4)**.

FIGURE 4

Assembly

10 Push the 8" (20.5 cm) wire tail through the hole in the Clay Cap.

11 Bend the wire 90 degrees so that it is laying flat against the Clay Cap.

12 Holding the wire stable with the round-nose pliers near the hole in the Clay Cap, begin coiling the wire around the hole (**Figure 5**), leaving a spot in the middle to add a polymer clay accent. When you have one complete coil, you can hold it stable with your finger as you continue coiling (**Figure 6**). When the spiral is the size you want, cut the end with flush cutters.

Finishing

COLOR RECIPE

ACCENT BEAD:

1 part turquoise polymer clay

¼ part white polymer clay

⅛ part gold polymer clay

13 Darken the wire with liver of sulfur (p. 19) and polish with #0000 steel wool.

14 Form a 10mm accent bead using the Accent Bead Color Recipe above.

15 Put a drop of liquid polymer clay onto the center of the cap and place the accent bead over it. If you want to have a flat top on the accent bead, press down on it with the Lucite square or other flat-surfaced object (**Figure 7**).

16 Cure for 30 minutes, then put into ice water for a few minutes. Dry off and apply the brown shoe polish to the accent bead with a firm paintbrush. Rub off excess shoe polish with a soft cloth or paper towel.

FIGURE 5

FIGURE 6

FIGURE 7

VARIATION IDEA

The polymer clay cap in the ring project is facing downward, but you can also assemble the ring with the cap facing upward. You may also find it easier to write on the inside of the cap because you can hold it on the outside while writing on the inside.

MOONDANCE
{ NECKLACE }

CIRCLES AND TEXTURES OVERLAP, COLLIDE, and dance together in this energetic celebration of color and form. A necklace such as this can be carefully planned, or you can let spontaneity determine the design. I like to make lots of pod shapes and rings with polymer clay and then play with them to see what combinations work best together.

Finished Size (of pendant): 2⅜ × 2¼" (6 × 5.5 cm)

MATERIALS

Polymer clay in black, white, translucent, red pearl, purple, orange, gold, and sea green

Liquid polymer clay

2' (61 cm) of 14-gauge sterling silver wire (or desired finished length plus 2" [5 cm])

2' (61 cm) of 16-gauge sterling silver wire

Brown shoe polish

Ice water

TOOLS

Acrylic roller or pasta machine

Light bulbs to use as molds; standard and 2" (5 cm) diameter decorative round

Extruder

Drinking straws in two different widths

Needle tool

Flat- or chain-nose pliers

Round-nose pliers

Flush cutters

Rubber mallet

Bench block and ball-peen hammer

Jeweler's file or paper manicurist file

2 different texture tools

Rubber thimble (also called a thimblette)

Latex gloves

Liver of sulfur

Firm paintbrush

#0000 steel wool

Soft polishing cloth

necklace

Lotus-Pod Pendant

FIGURE 1

COLOR RECIPES

SMALL POD:
1 part sea green polymer clay
1 part white polymer clay

LAVENDER RING:
1 part purple polymer clay
1 part translucent polymer clay
½ part white polymer clay

ORANGE RING:
1 part orange polymer clay
1 part translucent polymer clay
½ part white polymer clay
¼ part gold polymer clay

1   Make two cap-shaped elements on two light bulb molds. Use a larger (standard size) bulb and black polymer clay for the large pod; use a smaller bulb and the Color Recipe for the Small Pod above to mix the polymer clay for the small pod. Texture each of the pods, using a different texture for each (I used the rubber thimble for the large pod and a texture tip from the CoolTools Scatterbrained set for the small pod, **Figure 1**); set aside.

2   Roll two clay snakes, following the Color Recipes above for the Lavender Ring and then the Orange Ring. Do not blend the clay colors. Leaving them marbled will yield more aesthetically complex rings. Use unconditioned, old, or leeched clay if you want jagged edges on the rings. Flatten the clay snakes on a thin setting of the pasta machine or with an acrylic roller.

3   Form a ring from the lavender clay, using your fingers to gently coil the clay into a circle. Once you

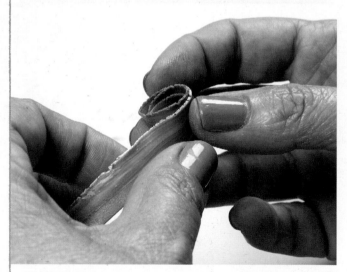

FIGURE 2

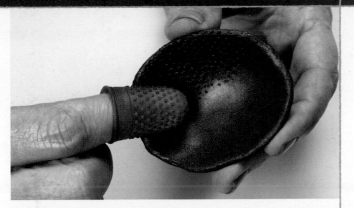

FIGURE 3

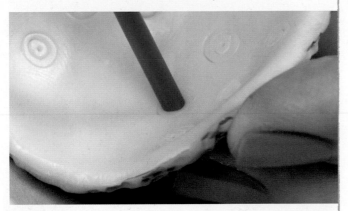

FIGURE 4

FIGURE 5

have a Lavender Ring, roll an Orange Ring around it; set aside (**Figure 2**).

4   Extrude a hollow cord of translucent clay to use as a channel for the wire neck cable on the back of the pendant. (Even though you will only need about a 1" [2.5 cm] piece, you may want to extrude a fairly long cord and cure it so you'll have it around for other uses.)

5   Cure the cap-shaped elements, the Lavender and Orange Ring, and the extruded cord for 15 minutes.

6   Make a flat sheet of red pearl polymer clay using the thickest setting on the pasta machine. After the pods are cooled, put a small amount of liquid polymer clay on the inside of the larger black one, add the flat sheet of red pearl polymer clay and press it down firmly, removing excess clay from the sides and blending it in. Texture the red clay with a rubber thimble (**Figure 3**).

7   Repeat Step 6 with the small pod but use translucent clay and do not texture. Smooth out any fingerprints with latex gloves and then embellish the pod by creating circle imprints with straws. Press the end of a straw into the clay to form a circle, then press a smaller straw into the middle of the circle just formed and finish by making a dot with a needle tool in the very center. Repeat all over the surface (**Figure 4**).

8   Cure both cap-shaped elements for 15 minutes. After they have cooled, apply shoe polish to both with a firm paintbrush. Rub off excess shoe polish with a soft cloth or paper towel.

9   Roll about 5 tiny balls of black polymer clay ranging in size from 1–3mm (the balls do not need to be uniform in size); set aside.

10 Fill the Lavender and Orange Ring element with translucent clay, blending it to create a smooth, flat surface (**Figure 5**).

11 Embellish the translucent surface just created with the black dots created in Step 8 by picking them up with the needle tool and placing them onto the translucent clay (**Figure 6**), then press them into the surface with your finger. Smooth away fingerprints by gently sliding your finger over the clay. You may find it easier if you moisten your finger with a drop of water (**Figure 7**).

12 Put a few drops of liquid polymer clay and a pea-sized piece of polymer clay into the bottom of the cap-shaped element, then place the smaller cap-shaped element on top to glue them together, forming the pendant (**Figure 8**).

13 Put a few drops of liquid polymer clay and a pea-sized piece of polymer clay into the bottom of the smaller cap-shaped element and press the lavender and orange ring onto it. Allow the elements to sit for about 24 hours before curing to form a stronger bond.

14 Cure for 15 minutes. Put into ice water for a few minutes, then dry off.

15 Attach the pendant's bail by laying about 1" (2.5 cm) of the translucent extruded cord onto the back of the pendant, centering it about ½" (1.3 cm) from the edge. Cover the cord with the black polymer clay to match the back of the pendant, leaving the hole at either end of the cord open so the pendant can later be hung on the neck cable. Blend the clay into the already-cured clay and texture it so it blends in seamlessly.

16 Cure for 40 minutes and cool.

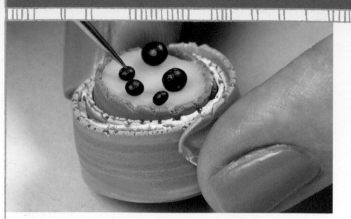

FIGURE 6

FIGURE 7

FIGURE 8

FIGURE 9

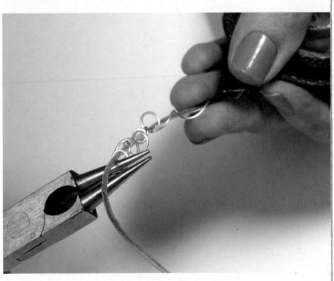

FIGURE 10

Neck Cable

TIP

Rather than trying to duplicate the freeform embellishment pictured on this necklace, improvise with your own loops and twists. It's a good idea to practice with craft or copper wire to get a sense of comfort with improvising with wire. Although it may be intimidating at first, with practice you'll find you not only loosen up, but actually enjoy it.

18 Cut a length of wire 2" (5 cm) longer than your desired completed length.

19 Lay the wire on the bench block and gently pound it with a mallet to work-harden and texture the wire.

20 Feed the wire through the bail on the back of the pendant.

21 Pound the ends of the wire with a hammer so they flare out and file them to eliminate any sharp points or edges.

22 Use round-nose pliers to form a loop about ¾" (2 cm) from one end of the wire, bending the wire back 180 degrees **(Figure 9)**. Repeat on the other end of the wire, forming the loop about 1" (2.5 cm) from the end of the wire and making sure to bend this second loop so that it is perpendicular to the first loop. The two loops will fit into each other to form a closure (see photo on p.100).

23 Add wire embellishment to the cable using two lengths of the 16-gauge wire. Be sure to flatten and file the ends, then use one piece of the wire on either side of the pendant, looping and coiling the wire as desired, using the round-nose and/or flat- or chain-nose pliers as needed, about halfway up the neck cable **(Figure 10)**. Secure the ends of the wire by wrapping tightly around the neck cable or looping as desired. Be sure the ends of the wire will not be poking into the neck of the wearer to ensure comfort.

24 Darken with liver of sulfur (p. 19), polish with #0000 steel wool and a soft polishing cloth.

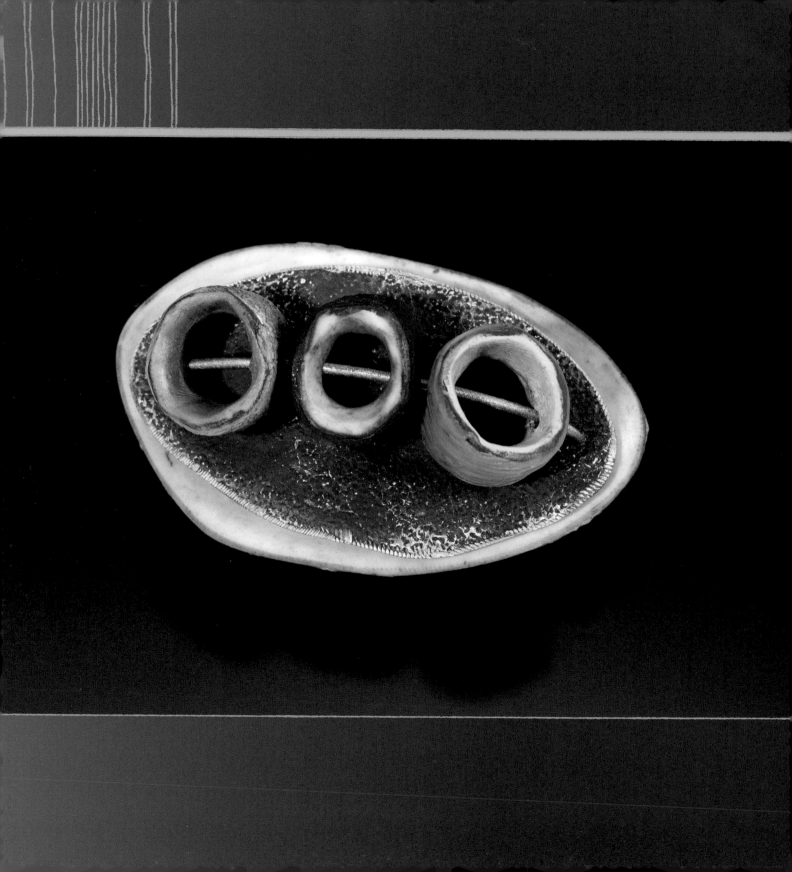

THREE-RING CIRCUS
{ BROOCH }

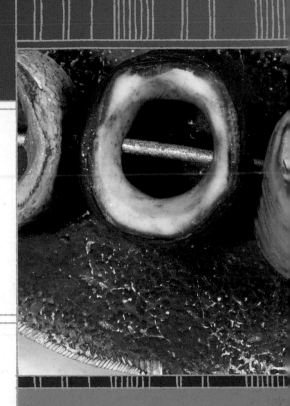

RINGS OF COLOR ASSERT THEMSELVES against a neutral background in this quirky composition. Polymer clay takes the starring role while the subtly textured wire plays a background role in the design. However, the wire is central to the construction, serving as a staple to hold the three rings in place. Brooches can embellish everyday objects such as scarves and hats, taking them from utilitarian to objets d'art.

Finished Size: 3 × 1¾" (7.5 × 4.5 cm)

MATERIALS

Polymer clay in black, white, translucent, purple, gold, crimson, orange, and turquoise

Liquid polymer clay

6" (15 cm) of sterling silver or copper 14-gauge wire

Sandpaper or other texturing material

Texture mats

White antiquing medium or white acrylic paint

Brown shoe polish

Pinch of cornstarch

Soft polishing cloth

1½" (3.8 cm) bar pin back

TOOLS

Pasta machine or acrylic roller

½" (1.3 cm) thin acrylic roller

Ring mandrel, polymer clay ring blank (see Tip on p. 109), or wooden dowel

Linoleum cutters

Jeweler's metal file

Flush cutters

Liver of sulfur

#0000 steel wool

brooch

Foundation Ovals

1. Form a 30–35 mm ball of translucent polymer clay, distort it slightly, and run it through the thickest setting of the pasta machine to achieve an irregular oval shape. If the oval shape is pleasing, lay it on a piece of paper to cure it (if you aren't happy with the shape, repeat the process until you achieve the desired shape; **Figure 1**).

2. Repeat the process with a slightly smaller ball of black clay. Texture with sandpaper.

3. Cure the ovals for 40 minutes.

4. After the ovals have cured, rub a file against the edge of the translucent oval to texture the edge and then apply shoe polish to the translucent oval with a firm paintbrush. Be sure to rub the shoe polish into the edge indentations so the texture is more pronounced. Rub off excess with a soft cloth or paper towel.

5. Use a cloth, paintbrush, or your fingers to rub some white antiquing pigment or acrylic paint over the black oval, pushing it into the crevasses (**Figure 2**), and then rub it away from the surface with a cloth or paper towel while it is still wet, letting the pigment remain in the crevasses (**Figure 3**).

6. Cure for another 10 minutes to "heat-set" the pigment.

FIGURE 1

FIGURE 2

FIGURE 3

Rings

COLOR RECIPES

LEFT RING:

OUTSIDE BAND:
4 parts white polymer clay
1 part purple polymer clay
¼ part black polymer clay

INSIDE BAND:
Gold polymer clay

CENTER RING:

OUTSIDE BAND:
Crimson polymer clay

INSIDE BAND:
Translucent polymer clay

RIGHT RING:

OUTSIDE BAND:
ORANGE POLYMER CLAY

INSIDE BAND:
1 part turquoise polymer clay
1 part white polymer clay

TIP

Rings can be formed over a ring mandrel, a wooden dowel,
or a polymer clay ring blank. If you want to make a polymer
clay ring blank, roll a log of clay at least 1" (2.5 cm) long × the
diameter you want your ring to be. Cure the ring blank for 45
minutes.

7   Roll a sheet of black clay on the thickest setting of the pasta machine. Cut it into three strips, each 3" (7.5 cm) long × ¾" (2 cm) wide. Use the strips to form three rings on a dowel, polymer clay ring mold, or ring mandrel that has been dusted with cornstarch. Blend the seams of the rings with the ½" (1.3 cm) thin acrylic roller.

8   Cure for 15 minutes and cool.

9   After the rings have cooled, roll a thin sheet of clay for each of the Inside Bands, following the Color Recipes above. Lay the thin sheets of clay onto the insides of the rings. You may find it easier to do this with separate pieces, blending them together after they have been patted down onto the inside of the ring. Pat the polymer clay down so it adheres and rub away the excess clay from the sides (**Figure 4**).

10 Cure for 15 minutes.

11 Add polymer clay to the outside of each ring by rolling a thin sheet of clay for each of the Outside Bands, following the Color Recipes above, cutting them into rectangular strips and blending them onto the outside of the rings. After the clay has been affixed to the ring, texture each of the three rings differently with the texture mats (**Figure 5**).

12 Cure rings for 25 minutes and cool.

13 Using a linoleum cutter, cut holes large enough for the 14-gauge wire to pass through the sides of the rings (**Figure 6**).

14 Apply brown shoe polish to the cured rings with a firm paintbrush and then remove the excess with a soft cloth or paper towel.

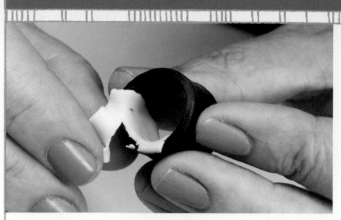

FIGURE 4

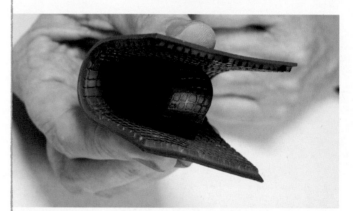

FIGURE 5

FIGURE 6

FIGURE 7

FIGURE 8

Wire

15 Slightly texture the 14-gauge wire by rubbing it with sandpaper or a file.

16 Darken the wire with liver of sulfur (p. 19) and then polish with #0000 steel wool and a polishing cloth.

Assembling the Brooch

17 String (p. 129) the three rings onto the wire. Holding the three rings close together, position them on the smaller black Foundation Oval. Mark two spots on the foundation oval, one on each outer edge of the two outside rings, with a carving tool or a permanent marker. This will be where the wire will go through.

18 Use a linoleum cutter to cut holes through the Foundation Oval at the spots you have marked (**Figure 7**).

19 Place the translucent oval under the black oval and cut through the holes in the translucent oval, using the black oval's holes as a guide.

20 Feed 1" (2.5 cm) of the wire through the holes on one end and form a wire staple by bending it against the back of the oval facing toward the middle (**Figure 8**).

21 Slide the rings up against the wire where it has been fed through the hole and feed the other end of the wire through the holes on the other end of the ovals. Trim it to 1" (2.5 cm) and bend it toward the middle, finishing the wire staple **(Figure 9)**.

22 Roll out a sheet of translucent polymer clay on a medium setting of the pasta machine. Coat the back of the translucent Foundation Oval with liquid polymer clay and then lay the translucent clay sheet over it (Figure 10). Press down firmly, then tear away the extra clay at the edges with your fingers and smooth the edge.

23 Lay the pin back on the back of the translucent oval. Roll out a piece of translucent clay and lay it over the pin back so it is covered in clay. Blend the clay with your fingers until it is seamlessly blended with the rest of the translucent oval, then texture the entire oval with a texture pad **(Figure 10)**.

24 Cure for 40 minutes.

25 Apply brown shoe polish to the cured translucent clay with a firm paintbrush and then rub off the excess with a soft cloth or paper towel **(Figure 11)**.

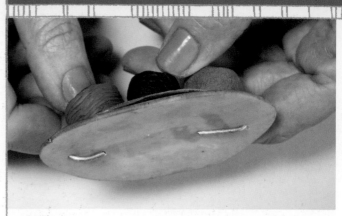

FIGURE 9

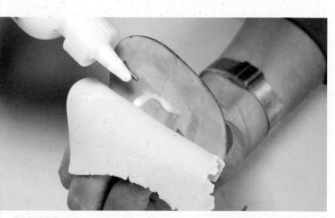

FIGURE 10

FIGURE 10

FIGURE 11

TERIOSITY Circles and orbs are universally pleasing and appropriate for many jewelry applications. The podlike focal on this bracelet would be equally successful as a pin . . . or the pendant of a necklace.

SO MUCH AND MORE
{ BRACELET }

WHO KNEW THAT A SIMPLE LENGTH OF EXTRUDED POLYMER CLAY could be the basis for such a beautiful bracelet? The wire embellishment not only provides a striking counterpoint, but it works as an artistic tension clasp, with the ends fitting snugly into the polymer clay bangle. Serendipity plays a role in this bracelet as well because what emerges from the extruder is always slightly different.

Finished Size: 8" (20.5 cm) circumference

MATERIALS

Polymer clay in white, translucent, orange, fuchsia, gold, and violet

Liquid polymer clay

8" (20.5 cm) of 14-gauge copper wire

Ice water

TOOLS

Acrylic roller

Tissue blade

Extruder

Flat- or chain-nose pliers

Round-nose pliers

Flush cutters

Soft polishing cloth

bracelet

COLOR RECIPE

BRACELET:

1 part orange polymer clay

1 part fuchsia polymer clay

1 part white polymer clay

1 part translucent polymer clay

1 part gold polymer clay

ACCENT:

1 part orange polymer clay

1 part violet polymer clay

1 part translucent polymer clay

FIGURE 1

FIGURE 2

FIGURE 3

1 Divide each bracelet color (see the Bracelet Color Recipe above) into four pieces (if you would like to achieve cracked edges as in the photo on p. 114, be sure that your clay is not too conditioned). Put bracelet colors into extruder, alternating the colors to achieve more variation in the bangle. Do not blend the colors before putting them into the extruder—they will get blended in the process of being extruded.

2 Fit the extruder with the large core attachment and the square disk. Choose a core attachment that is the same size as the 14-gauge wire (check the size by holding the wire up to the core attachment [**Figure 1**]).

3 Extrude the four-sided cord (**Figure 2**).

4 Cut the cord down to about 7" (18 cm) or a little less than the desired finished length (the clasp will add about 1" [2.5 cm]) and form into an oval on a sheet of paper (**Figure 3**). Cure for 20 minutes.

5 Mix clay for the accent according to the Accent Color Recipe above. Form two 8mm balls.

6 After the extruded bracelet form has cooled, put a drop of liquid polymer clay on one end and add one of the 8mm balls of accent clay, pressing it onto the bracelet end. Use a scrap piece of 14-gauge wire to

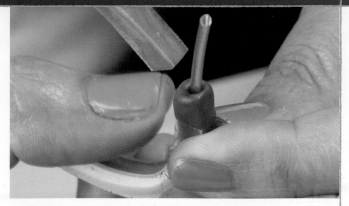

FIGURE 4

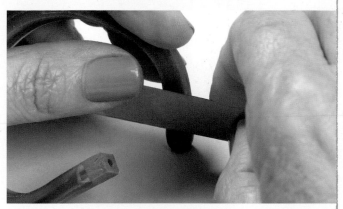

FIGURE 5

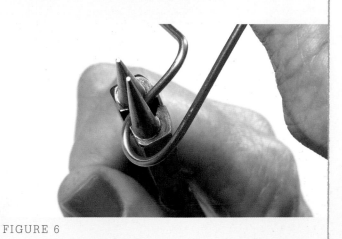

FIGURE 6

poke a hole about ½" (1.3 cm) long into the accent clay so it has a core in it (**Figure 4**). Repeat entire step on the other end of the bracelet.

7   Pat the end of the unbaked ball of clay so the end is smooth and straight and repeat on the other side. Don't bother trying to get the sides even—it's too hard to achieve crisp edges on uncured clay (see Step 8 to achieve crisp edges).

8   Cure again for 15 minutes. After it has cooled, use the tissue blade to slice off the extra polymer clay so the accent is flush with the rest of the extruded bracelet (**Figure 5**).

9   Cure for 40 minutes.

Create Clasp

10   Cut an 8" (20.5 cm) length of 14-gauge wire.

11   Leaving a 1" (2.5 cm) tail, bend a 90-degree angle in the wire with round-nose pliers. This tail will fit into one side of the bracelet core.

12   Grasp the wire with flat- or chain-nose pliers and loosely loop the wire in a couple different directions to create a free-form embellishment. You may want to use round-nose pliers to form some loops. There is no right or wrong—you are just bending the wire in different directions to create an interesting sculptural element (**Figure 6**).

13   Trim the wire at each end to leave a ½" (1.3 cm) tail on each side. Bend the ends of the wire so they fit into the ends of the bracelet while the wire embellishment stays above them. File the ends of the wire so there are no sharp points.

14   Darken the wire with liver of sulfur (p. 19) and polish with #0000 steel wool and then a soft polishing cloth.

15   The two ends of the wire fit snugly into the ends of the bracelet, serving as the focal embellishment. One end can be pulled out when putting on and taking off the bracelet and then inserted back into the bangle to form a tension clasp.

EMBRACE ME
{ RING }

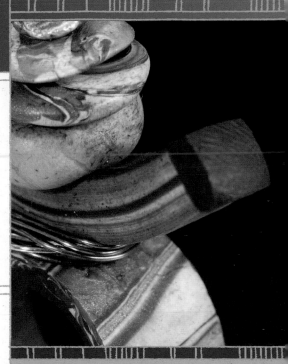

THIS PIECE TAKES THE CONCEPT OF A COCKTAIL RING to new places. One of the most common mistakes jewelry designers make is putting a heavy focal element on a ring shank that isn't substantial enough for it, so the focal element slips to the side instead of staying upright. Fortunately, polymer clay is lightweight, so you can get away with making an outrageously large focal element just for fun.

Finished Size: 2 × 2¾" (5 × 7 cm)

MATERIALS

Polymer clay in black, white, translucent, turquoise, gold, and crimson

Liquid polymer clay

6" (15 cm) of sterling silver 22-gauge wire

1 silver 6–8mm embellishment bead

1 silver 2" (50 mm) ball-end head pin

Cornstarch

Brown shoe polish

Aluminum foil (about 1 × 1' [30.5 × 30.5 cm])

Ice water

TOOLS

Pasta machine or acrylic roller

½" (1.3 cm) thin acrylic roller

Needle tool

Tissue blade

2" (5 cm) round decorative light bulb to use as a mold

Extruder

Ring mandrel, wooden dowel, or polymer clay ring blank (see Step 10 on p. 121)

Linoleum cutter

Flush cutters

Chain-nose pliers

Liver of sulfur

#0000 steel wool

Firm paintbrush

Polishing cloth

Ring

Focal Elements

COLOR RECIPE

EXTRUDED CLAY:
1 part white polymer clay
1 part turquoise polymer clay
1 part gold polymer clay
1 part translucent polymer clay
¼ part black polymer clay
⅛ part crimson polymer clay

ACCENT BEAD:
1 part turquoise polymer clay
½ part white polymer clay
½ part translucent polymer clay
A tiny pinch of black polymer clay

1   Following the Color Recipe for the Extruded Clay above, put polymer clay into an extruder with the square disk attachment to make a four-sided extrusion. The polymer clay should not be blended before it is placed into the extruder; it will blend together as it is extruded. Be sure to extrude enough for both the arc-shaped focal element and the ring shank.

2   Cut off 2" (5 cm) of the extrusion and form it into an arc on a light-bulb mold **(Figure 1)**; cure for 15 minutes.

3   After the extruded arc has cooled, look it over to see if you have any favorite part where the marbling is particularly intriguing. Use the tissue blade to cut it down to about 1½" (3.8 cm), making sure your favorite part remains.

4   Form two 8mm balls of clay from the crimson clay.

FIGURE 1

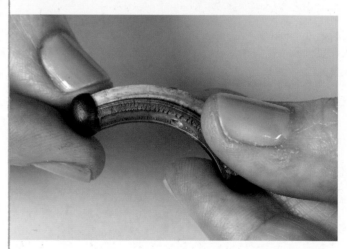

FIGURE 2

FIGURE 3

FIGURE 4

FIGURE 5

5   Put a drop of liquid polymer clay on one end of the arc and add one of the 8mm balls (from Step 4). Pat the end so it is smooth and straight and repeat on the other side. Don't bother trying to get the sides even just yet **(Figure 2)**.

6   Cure again for 15 minutes. After it has cooled, use the tissue blade to slice off the extra polymer clay so the accent is flush with the rest of the extruded arc; set aside **(Figure 3)**.

7   Form a 12mm round accent bead using the Color Recipe for the Accent Bead on p. 124. Place the bead onto the arc and flatten the bead slightly by gently pressing down on it so the bottom conforms to the shape of the arc. Remove the bead from the arc for curing.

8   Using scraps of clay from the extruded arc, form two disks, one about 10mm wide and the other about 12mm wide.

9   Cure the accent bead and disks for 25 minutes; set aside.

Ring Shank

10   Rings can be formed over a ring mandrel, a wooden dowel, or a polymer clay ring blank. If you want to make a polymer clay ring blank, roll a log of clay at least 1" (2.5 cm) long × the diameter you want your ring to be. Cure for 45 minutes.

11   Press the remaining extruded clay flat, cut it into 4" (10 cm) strips and press them together to form a sheet about 4" (10 cm) long × 1" (2.5 cm) wide **(Figure 4)**.

12   Run the sheet through a medium-thick setting of the pasta machine.

13   Cut a long rectangular strip from the sheet that equals the desired measurement of the rink shank.

14   Put some cornstarch on the ring mandrel, wooden dowel, or polymer clay ring blank to act as a release agent, and wrap the rectangular strip of polymer clay around it **(Figure 5)**.

15 Make a straight cut where the edges of the clay strip meet up and gently blend the two edges together with the ½" (1.3 cm) thin acrylic roller to join them **(Figure 6)**.

16 With a tissue blade, trim the edges of the ring shank to the desired width **(Figure 7)**.

17 Cure for 15 minutes and cool.

18 After the ring shank has cooled, roll a thin sheet of crimson polymer clay. Lay the thin sheet of clay onto the inside of the ring shank. Pat it down so it adheres and rub away the excess clay from the sides. You may find it easier to do with separate pieces, blending them together after they've been patted down onto the inside of the ring. **(Figure 8)**.

19 Cure for 15 minutes.

Assembling the Ring

20 Using a linoleum cutter, make a small hole through the middle of each of the Focal Elements (created in Steps 1–9).

21 String the Focal Elements onto the ball-end head pin in the following order: sterling silver accent bead, both clay disks, 12mm clay Accent Bead, and the extruded arc. Snug the Focal Elements together, then form a sharp 90-degree bend in the head pin with your finger at the base of the arc to hold the elements firmly together. Cut the wire, leaving only about ⅛" (3 mm).

22 It is important to use plenty of liquid polymer clay and uncured clay to attach the Focal Elements to the ring shank so the ring will not pull apart if it is bumped (and since rings are on hands, they do get lots of abuse). Put a generous amount of liquid polymer clay on the ring shank, add a small scrap of uncured polymer clay, add another few drops of liquid polymer clay and press the focal element onto the ring shank **(Figure 9)**.

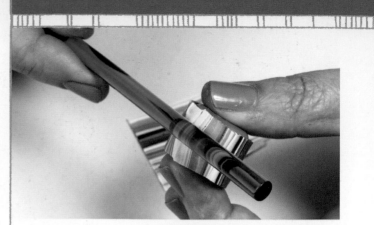

FIGURE 6

FIGURE 7

FIGURE 8

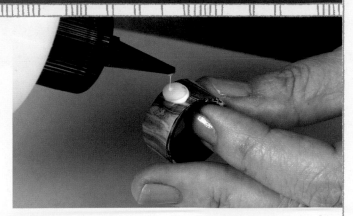

FIGURE 9

FIGURE 10

23 Because you are using a generous amount of poly- mer clay and liquid polymer clay to "glue" the ele- ments together, some may squish out as you press. Use the needle tool to remove some of the excess. Allow the elements to sit for about 24 hours before curing, to allow the liquid polymer clay to form a stronger bond.

24 It may be necessary to build a temporary propping mechanism to hold the ring upright while it is cur- ing so the focal element doesn't come loose from the ring shank. You can do this quickly and easily by crumpling up some aluminum foil around the ring and resting it on the foil while it cures. Cure for 45 minutes, put into ice water for a few minutes, then dry off.

25 Apply brown shoe polish to the entire ring with a firm paintbrush and then rub off the excess with a soft cloth or paper towel.

26 Wrap wire around the glued connection between the ring shank and the Focal Elements. The wire will stay attached more snugly if you leave a tail at both ends, then wind the two wire tails around each other and pull firmly so the wire is tied to the base (**Figure 10**).

Continue wrapping the wire so it is completely wrapped around the connection. Tuck the wire end in with chain-nose pliers.

VARIATION IDEA

Make your own polymer clay-tipped head pins by making a loop or some other small bend at the end of a piece of wire so it will "grab onto" the clay and then cover it with a tiny ball of clay. Cure for 20 minutes and you have an embellished head pin, which would be fun to use in place of a silver-tipped head pin.

ANCIENT VESSEL
{ NECKLACE }

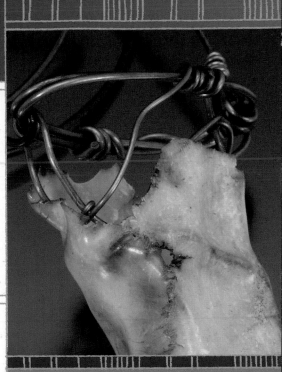

I'VE ALWAYS BEEN FASCINATED WITH ANCIENT ARTIFACTS. I find old things that are missing pieces or parts particularly engaging. What is missing? What did it look like when it was new? The pendant on this necklace, with its polymer clay membrane covering only a part of its frame, invites those looking at it to wonder what is missing and take a closer look at what remains.

Finished Size (of pendant): 2 × 2¾" (5 × 7 cm)

MATERIALS

Translucent polymer clay

Brown shoe polish

10' (3 m) of sterling silver or copper 18-gauge wire

6" (15.5 cm) of sterling silver or copper 22-gauge wire

32" (81.5 cm) of black 2mm leather cord

Polyester fiberfill quilt batting

TOOLS

Pasta machine or acrylic roller

Needle tool

Flat-nose or chain-nose pliers

Round-nose pliers

Flush cutters

Liver of sulfur

#0000 steel wool

Firm paintbrush

Soft polishing cloth

necklace

Wire-Basket Frame

Note: Rather than trying to estimate how much wire you'll need for a rim, begin by bending the wire from a coil of wire. You don't need to bend it in the exact shape you'll want since you'll be shaping it as you work.

1. Using your fingers, work the wire into an oval shape about 2½" (6.5 cm) long × 1" (2.5 cm) wide for the rim of the basket frame. Continue working the wire to form a double loop. Leave a wire tail of about 2" (5 cm) to coil around the rim. Since this basket is free-form, you may want to leave a longer tail to make a longer and/or looser coil **(Figure 1)**.

2. Use the tail end of the wire to wrap around the rim, holding the coils in place.

3. Create wire ribs to add structure to the basket frame, by adding wire from a coil of wire, forming a U-shaped rib running perpendicular to the rim **(Figure 2)**. You will be shaping the rib more as you form the basket, so the shape doesn't need to be exact, but you do need to work (or play!) with it to get the size of frame you want. You can aim for long and thin or short and boxy, so indulge your creativity.

4. Once you've formed a U-shaped rib, flush cut the wire, leaving a tail long enough to form another U-shaped rib plus an extra 4" (10 cm) to anchor it onto the rim on the opposite side of the rim from the beginning of the U-shaped rib just formed.

5. Repeat Step 3, making another U-shaped rib that crosses the first on the bottom of the basket frame. Be sure to loop the working wire around the first U-shaped rib at the bottom to anchor the two ribs together where they cross **(Figure 3)**.

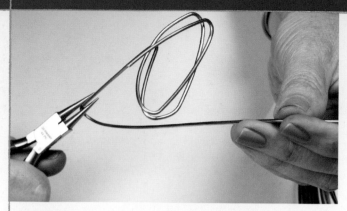

FIGURE 1

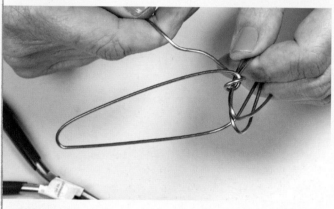

FIGURE 2

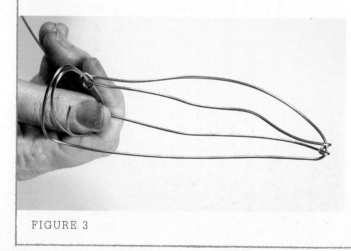

FIGURE 3

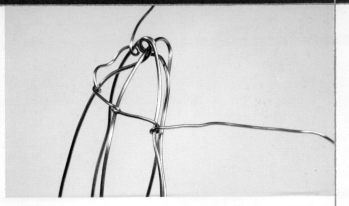

FIGURE 4

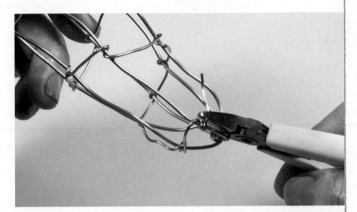

FIGURE 5

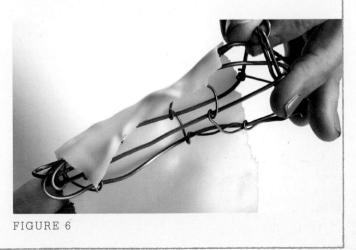

FIGURE 6

6 Cut a piece of wire long enough to wrap around the vertical ribs a few times (about 4' [1.2 m]). Coil one end of it around the bottom of the basket a few times, where the vertical ribs meet, to hold them together and to anchor the wire (**Figure 4**).

7 Wrap the wire around one of the vertical ribs once to attach. Now you can begin to build horizontal spokes by wrapping the wire around the vertical ribs, making one loop around each rib to anchor the wire firmly in place. Continue wrapping. Flush-cut the remaining tail of wire where you began wrapping the horizontal spokes (**Figure 5**).

8 Finish off by wrapping the end of the tail around the rim to secure. Oxidize with liver of sulfur (p. 19).

Membrane

9 Roll a sheet of translucent clay on the thinnest setting of the pasta machine.

10 Lay the clay over the basket. Tear the edges to form a rough edge and gently pat the clay onto the basket so the clay adheres to the wire (**Figure 6**). You do not need to encircle the whole basket; you will cover the second half of the frame in Step 13. This will allow you to adhere the clay to the frame securely.

11 Gently pinch the clay edges onto some of the wire basket ribs so it encloses the ribs (**Figure 7**).

12 Place the basket on a piece of fiberfill and cure for 15 minutes.

13 After the basket has cooled, roll another sheet of translucent clay, as in Step 9, and add it to the basket so it is encircled in clay and so that the edges of the clay overlap slightly.

14 Put a few drops of liquid polymer clay on the edge of the cured clay and join the pieces together by making little hash marks with a needle tool directly over the "seam" where the two pieces meet (**Figure 8**).

ANCIENT VESSEL NECKLACE

15 Place the basket on a piece of fiberfill and cure for 25 minutes.

16 Put into ice water for a few minutes to make the translucent clay more translucent. Apply the shoe polish to the translucent clay with a firm paintbrush and then rub off the excess with a soft cloth or paper towel (**Figure 9**).

Attach Leather Cord

17 Oxidize the 22-gauge copper or sterling silver wire with liver of sulfur (p. 19).

18 Loop leather cord through the rim. Firmly coil 3" (8 cm) of the oxidized wire around the leather to hold the loop (**Figure 10**; be sure to oxidize the wire prior to using it on the leather cord to avoid dipping the leather into liver of sulfur). Repeat entire step to attach the other end of the leather cord to the other side of the rim. Be sure to use a length of leather cord that is long enough to fit over your head.

19 Carefully buff the wire coils with fine steel wool, taking care not to damage the leather surrounding the coil, and polish with a soft cloth.

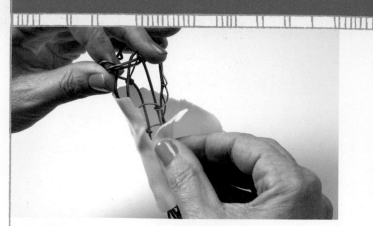

FIGURE 7

FIGURE 8

FIGURE 9

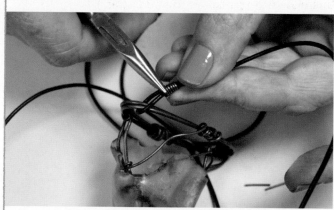

FIGURE 10

GLOSSARY

SIMPLE LOOP

Use flat-nose pliers to make a 90-degree bend at least ½"
(1.3 cm) from the end of the wire **(Figure 1)**. Use round-
nose pliers to grasp the wire after the bend; roll the pliers
toward the bend, but not past it, to preserve the 90-degree
bend. Use your thumb to continue the wrap around the
nose of the pliers **(Figure 1)**. Trim the wire next to the
bend **(Figure 1)**.

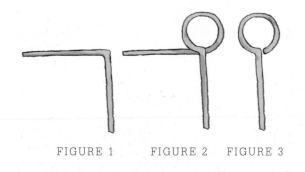

FIGURE 1   FIGURE 2   FIGURE 3

STRINGING

Stringing is a technique in which you use beading wire or
other material to gather beads into a strand.

OPENING AND CLOSING A JUMP RING

Open a jump ring by grasping each side of its opening
with a pair of pliers (chain- and/or flat-nose pliers); don't
pull apart. Instead, twist in opposite directions to avoid
distorting the shape. To close a jump ring, twist each side
back together until the two edges meet.

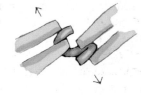

OVERHAND KNOT

Make a loop with the stringing material. Pass the cord
that lies behind the loop over the front cord, then through
the loop and pull snug.

DOUBLE OVERHAND KNOT

To make a double overhand knot, tie an overhand knot
with the stringing material, then tie a second overhand
knot directly over the first one.

GALLERY

Polymer clay and wire are both astonishingly versatile materials. Here are a few more examples of what you can do with a few tools, a bit of clay and wire, and a desire to play and create. The combinations that emerge can be striking and unexpected.

Light the Dark—This piece utilizes hollow-cored elements, made by using a core attachment in the extruder. The dense matte texture on the black elements is achieved with extremely fine-grade sandpaper.

String Theory—Since polymer clay assumes the texture it's molded on, the inside of these pods are as smooth and shiny as a light bulb. The guitar strings placed in the center are an amusing addition to this brooch.

Hurry to Here—A beautiful hand-dyed silk cord was the color inspiration for this idiosyncratic necklace. Dark wire offsets the cool hues of the polymer clay focal and silk cord for a stunning visual effect.

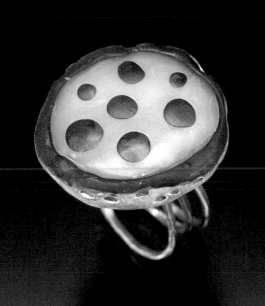

The Wanderer—Although red and orange appear next to each other on the color wheel and therefore conventional wisdom would say they are a serene combination, I find the combination to be one of the most energetic, particularly when coupled with black and white.

Behold the Sight—Who says a clasp needs to sit behind the wearer's neck? The undulating textured wire embellishment fits snugly into hollow Softglas cord and serves as a clasp that is just off-center, near the pendant.

Slightly Mad—Never underestimate the versatility of a needle tool, which was used to create tiny dots on the green pod and carve rough grooves into the yellow orb near the center.

Randy's Daydream—Clay extruded out of a tiny hole in the extruder adds a fiberlike contrast to the marbled clay in this playful ring.

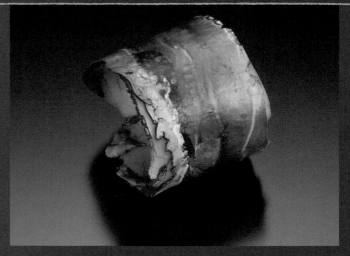

Edge of a Song—Clay that was leeched before it was marbled yielded the stunning rough edges of this bangle. There's something about gold polymer clay that makes a piece sing.

What's Black and White . . .?—Only black, white, and translucent polymer clays were used to make the beads in this necklace, but the variety of shapes, textures, and embellishments keep it engaging. Adding a touch of brown shoe polish gives the necklace a resonant patina.

Claire le Lune—This striking pendant evokes the sensuality of an ancient corset. A simple monochromatic silk cord ensures that all the attention is focused on the main attraction.

Exotic Idea—A heavy application of shoe polish yielded deep brown tones. Although only black, white, and translucent polymer clay were used, the shoe polish brought out rich color to highlight the circles and dots.

Hope's Jubilation—One of my favorite design elements is intrigue. The white bead with large black circles peeking out from the bead caps in the focal element adds to the charm of this piece by engaging the viewer with a question "What's hidden in here?"

RESOURCES

SUPPLIERS

Polymer Clay Express
*Comprehensive polymer clay supply
(including Lucite squares)*
polymerclayexpress.com
Polymer Clay Express at
TheArtWay Store
9890 Main St.
Damascus, MD 20872
(800) 844-0138

Cool Tools
*Comprehensive precious metal clay
supply, including many exclusive tools for
polymer clay*
cooltools.us
162 West Main St., Ste. M
Whitewater, WI 53190
(888) 478-5060

Jatayu
*Wire and metalworking tools, supplies,
and jewelry from wire artist Connie Fox*
jatayu.com
(888) 350-6481

Objects and Elements
*Jewelry supply and more (including heishi
spacers)*
objectsandelements.com
23216 E. Echo Lake Rd.
Snohomish, WA 98296
(206) 965-0373

Somerset Silver
*Hill tribe silver from Thailand (including
the silver beads used in projects)*
somerset-silver.com
PO Box 253
Mukilteo, WA 98275
(425) 641-3666

The Carving Glove Guy
High-quality carving tools
thecarvinggloveguy.com
7870 Parker Rd.
Saline, MI 48176
(734) 944-1918

Rio Grande
Comprehensive jewelry supply
riogrande.com
7500 Bluewater Rd. NW
Albuquerque, NM 87121
(800) 545-6566

Thunderbird Supply Company
Comprehensive jewelry supply
thunderbirdsupply.com
1907 W. Historic Rt. 66
Gallup, NM 87301
(505) 722-4323

Polyform Products
Manufacturers of PREMO polymer clay
sculpey.com
1901 Estes Ave.
Elk Grove Village, IL 60007
(847) 427-0020

Jacquard Products
Inks, paints, and other supplies
jacquardproducts.com
PO Box 425
Healdsburg, CA 95448
(800) 442-0455

ONLINE EDUCATION AND INSPIRATION

International Polymer Clay Association
npcg.org

Glass Attic
*An extensive online database of
polymer clay techniques*
glassattic.com

Polymer Clay Daily
polymerclaydaily.com

Daily Art Muse
dailyartmuse.com

COLOR COOKBOOKS

*Color Harmony: A Guide to Creative Color
Combinations* (Paperback)
by Hideako Chijiiwa

*Color Index: Over 1100 Color Combina-
tions, CMYK and RGB Formulas, for Print
and Web Media* (Turtleback)
by Jim Krause

RONNA'S JEWELRY

ronnasarvasweltman.com

Thanks to Chanh Nguyen for doing the
math for the coiling chart on p. 21.

INDEX

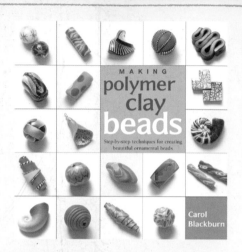
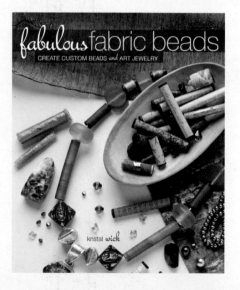